Cleopatra: Egypt's Last Pharaoh

Don Nardo
AR B.L.: 9.9
Points: 6.0

LUCENT LIBRARY *of* HISTORICAL ERAS

CLEOPATRA
EGYPT'S LAST PHARAOH

DON NARDO

LUCENT BOOKS

An imprint of Thomson Gale, a part of The Thomson Corporation

THOMSON
─────✷─────
GALE

™

Detroit • New York • San Francisco • San Diego • New Haven, Conn. • Waterville, Maine • London • Munich

LIBRARY OF CONGRESS CATALOGING-IN-PUBLICATION DATA

Nardo, Don, 1947–
    Cleopatra: Egypt's Last Pharaoh / By Don Nardo.
        p. cm. — (Lucent library of historical eras. Ancient Egypt)
    Includes bibliographical references and index.
    ISBN 1-59018-660-5 (hardcover : alk. paper)
    1. Cleopatra, Queen of Egypt, d. 30 B.C.—Juvenile literature. 2. Egypt—History—332–30 B.C.—Juvenile literature. 3. Queens—Egypt—Biography—Juvenile literature. I. Title. II. Series.
    DT92.7.N37 2005
    932'.021'092—dc22
                                                                2004022071

Printed in the United States of America

Contents

Foreword

Looking back from the vantage point of the present, history can be viewed as a myriad of intertwining roads paved by human events. Some paths stand out—broad highways whose mileposts, even from a distance of centuries, are clear. The events that propelled the rise to power of Germany's Third Reich, its role in World War II, and its eventual demise, for example, are well defined and documented.

Other roads are less distinct, their route sometimes hidden from view. Modern legislatures may have developed from old tribal councils, for example, but the links between them are indistinct in places, open to discussion and interpretation.

The architecture of civilization—law, religion, art, science, and government—as well as the more everyday aspects of our culture—what we eat, what we wear—all developed along the historical roads and byways. In that progression can be traced every facet of modern life.

A broad look back along these roads reveals that many paths—though of vastly different character—seem to converge at a few critical junctions. These intersections are those great historical eras that echo over the long, steady course of human history, extending beyond the past and into the present.

These epic periods of time are the focus of Lucent's Library of Historical Eras. They shine through the mists of history like beacons, illuminated by a burst of creativity that propels events forward—so bright that we, from thousands of years away, can clearly see the chain of events leading to the present.

Each Lucent Library of Historical Eras consists of a set of books that highlight various aspects of these major eras. For example, the Elizabethan England library features volumes on Queen Elizabeth I and her court, Elizabethan theater, the great playwrights, and everyday life in Elizabethan London.

The mini-library approach allows for the division of each era into its most significant and most interesting parts and the exploration of those parts in depth. Also, social and cultural trends as well as illustrative documents and eyewitness accounts can be prominently featured in individual volumes.

Lucent's Library of Historical Eras presents a wealth of information to young readers. The lively narrative, fully documented primary and secondary source quotations, maps, photographs, sidebars, and annotated bibliographies serve as launching points for class discussion and further research.

In studying the great historical eras, students also develop a better understanding of our own times. What we learn from the past and how we apply it in the present may shape the future and may determine whether our era will be a guiding light to those traveling future roads.

THE DISTORTING MIRRORS OF CLEOPATRA'S REFLECTION

Noted classical scholar Peter Green once memorably remarked that Cleopatra VII, last of the Egyptian pharaohs, has long exercised a "mesmeric [hypnotic] fascination . . . upon the European [Western] imagination."[1] Indeed, Cleopatra was a larger-than-life figure in her own time (the late first century B.C., as tens of millions of people either despised her or held her in awe. And following her untimely death (by suicide) in 30 B.C., her legend continued to grow.

Like all famous and mysterious figures of the past, Cleopatra became a sort of magnet that attracted writers and artists of all types in each new generation. In medieval and modern times her exploits were revisited and often greatly embellished in countless paintings, poems, plays, novels, and movies. In this way, there became in a sense many different Cleopatras, each shaped in the mind's eye of the beholder or interpreter. On the one hand, "she is a pattern of female virtue," her modern biographer Lucy Hughes-Hallett points out, and on the other "she is a sexual glutton."

She is a true and tender lover who died for her man. She is a royal princess whose courage is proof of her nobility. She is an untrustworthy foreigner whose lasciviousness [sexual indecency] and cunning are typical of her race. She is a public benefactor, builder of aqueducts and lighthouses. She is a selfish tyrant who tortures

Opposite: Renaissance artist Michelangelo's sketch of Cleopatra is one of many by famous artists through the ages.

A statue of Cleopatra from her reign depicts her wearing the royal nemes *headdress.*

slaves for her entertainment. She is as playful as a child. She is as old as sin.[2]

Another modern writer, Théophile Gautier, has called the celebrated Egyptian queen "the most complete woman ever to have existed, the most womanly woman and the most queenly queen."[3] Yet some two thousand years before, the Roman poet Horace called her a "monstrous queen," the leader of a "loathsome herd of creatures vile with disease."[4]

Facts Clouded by Bias

The huge contrast between a modern writer's "queenly queen" and an ancient one's "monstrous queen" illustrates more than the wide variety of personal views of Cleopatra over the ages. It also highlights a serious problem that historians face when trying to compile factual chronicles of her life. Namely, almost all surviving writings about her, both ancient and modern, are romanticized to one degree or another. And it is a daunting task to separate fact from fiction in regard to her physical attributes, talents, and true accomplishments.

Perhaps the prime examples of this coloring and twisting of the facts are the works of the Greek and Roman writers who were contemporaries of Cleopatra or flourished in the generations immediately following her death. Besides Horace (first century B.C.), these included the Roman poet Virgil (first century B.C.); Roman naturalist and scholar Pliny the Elder (first century A.D.); Greek biographer Plutarch (first century A.D.); Greek historian Appian (second century A.D.); and Roman historian Dio Cassius (second century A.D.), among many others.

The works of some of these writers provide basic facts about Cleopatra. First and foremost, for instance, she was not an Egyptian (which inevitably surprises many people today). Instead, she was born a Macedonian Greek, a princess in the Ptolemaic line of rulers, those descended from the Greek general Ptolemy (pronounced TAW-luh-mee), who took control of Egypt in the late fourth century B.C. She deposed her younger brother and ascended the throne with the aid of the powerful Roman statesman Julius Caesar. They became lovers and allies. Later, after his death, she allied herself with another Roman leader, Marcus Antonius (now usually referred to as Mark Antony). Together, Cleopatra and Antony challenged Caesar's adopted son, Octavian, for control of the Roman world. Octavian was victorious, and Cleopatra killed herself. She was not only the last Egyptian pharaoh but also the last major autonomous Greek ruler of ancient times.

These are the principal and incontrovertible facts about Cleopatra's life. To some degree, the works of Plutarch, Dio Cassius, and a few others can be trusted with these and other basic events and other data. However, the more detail these ancient writers provide about the famous queen, the more slanted and unreliable their accounts become. This is partly because they tended to record hearsay and incorporate already existing tall tales about their subject. Also, they harbored an innate, deep-seated bias against any and all women

In this stone statue of Cleopatra, also from her reign, she wears the triple uraeus *crown.*

who were assertive, independent, and/or authority figures. And posterity subsequently absorbed and passed on this bias. "Cleopatra was Rome's enemy," writes Hughes-Hallett,

and we in the West are Rome's heirs. The notion of Cleopatra that we have inherited identifies her primarily as being the adversary, the Other. . . . Her Roman adversaries embody the "masculine" virtues of patriotism, discipline, sexual [restraint], and readiness for war.[5]

This explains Octavian's unconcealed disgust (as reported by Dio) at Rome being "trampled upon by a woman of Egypt," a situation that "disgraces our fathers." Dio duly reported Cleopatra's alliances with Caesar and Antony and the details of her final battle (at Actium in western Greece);

but he made sure to provide nearly equal space to Octavian's long-winded denunciation of "this pestilence of a woman." What decent Roman "would not tear his hair at the sight of Roman soldiers serving as bodyguards of this queen?"[6] Octavian asked his troops as they prepared to fight her at Actium.

A Veil of Mystery and Romance

Thus, in ancient times Cleopatra was widely seen as a threat to the established "natural" order in which men ruled and made policy and women knew their place. Her punishment for challenging this order was verbal attack, military defeat, death, the dissolution of her kingdom, and an eternal reputation as a scheming, power-hungry woman. Unfortunately, people in later generations, including the readers of this book, have been punished as well. The Romans who took over Ptolemaic Egypt made no effort to preserve governmental, legal, or other documents from Cleopatra's reign. In fact, the vast majority of such written evidence, which was probably at one time substantial, was purposely destroyed. And most of the other ancient factual data relating to Cleopatra, including her own writings (if any of those mentioned by ancient writers actually existed), were lost or simply disintegrated in the centuries that followed. Meanwhile, the exaggerated and often downright fabricated accounts and hearsay proliferated and flourished. And such mythmaking continues today.

The result is that modern historians, including the author of this volume, have appallingly little in the way of firm, documented evidence to use in reconstructing the legendary queen's life. They must try, where possible, to separate fact from fiction in the accounts of Plutarch, Dio, and others. And they frequently must digress and explore various political and cultural aspects of Cleopatra's world in hopes of shedding light on the forces that shaped and guided her.

The rest, by default, is educated speculation and, inescapably, to some degree a bit more mythmaking. As Hughes-Hallett points out, "Even the most scrupulous historian selects and edits," and each new book about Cleopatra, including even a straightforward history, becomes "yet another of the distorting mirrors in which Cleopatra's reflection appears tinted and reshaped by the glass which holds it."[7] This pattern seems likely to be repeated indefinitely. Unless some detailed, reliable records from Cleopatra's reign suddenly and miraculously materialize (a highly unlikely scenario), she will forever remain partially obscured by a veil of innuendo, propaganda, mystery, and romance.

Chapter One

CHILD OF PRIVILEGE: THE WORLD OF CLEOPATRA'S YOUTH

The last of ancient Egypt's pharaohs—Cleopatra VII—was born in the country's capital, Alexandria, in 69 B.C. Nothing specific is known about her life before she entered into a power struggle for the Egyptian throne at age nineteen or twenty (in 49 B.C.). However, it is possible to reconstruct the political situation, family background and structure, and physical and cultural settings of the era of her youth. These elements provide key clues to the people, city, palace, lifestyle, and political and family problems that she knew as a child.

Founding a New Dynasty

For example, tracing Cleopatra's lineage back several generations reveals how she ended up in a seemingly unlikely position—a young Greek woman who enjoyed a life of privilege in Egypt's royal palace and became heir to that country's throne. The Ptolemies, the royal family of which she

was a member, came to power in the following manner. Almost three centuries before Cleopatra's birth, Egypt, which had once been a mighty independent kingdom, languished under Persian rule. But in 332 B.C. the Macedonian Greek king and military adventurer Alexander III (later called "the Great") liberated Egypt. At least the Egyptians saw it as liberation. In truth, Alexander was in the midst of conquering the vast Persian realm, and all the lands wrenched away from the Persian king now became part of Alexander's own empire.

Perhaps Alexander's most lasting contribution to Egypt was his founding of the city of Alexandria. Located in the western reaches of the Nile Delta on the Mediterranean coast, it rapidly became one of the leading ports and commercial centers of the known world. It also replaced Egypt's older cities of Memphis and Thebes as the nation's capital. Alexander witnessed none of these far-reaching developments, however. Shortly after approving the layout of the new city and hiring the chief architect, he departed Egypt to continue his subjugation of Persia. After completing this monumental task, he died quite suddenly (perhaps of alcohol poisoning) in 323 B.C.

The problem was that Alexander, who in the short space of a decade had amassed the largest empire ever seen, had not named an heir. As a result, his leading generals became embroiled in a bitter and bloody power struggle that lasted for more than a generation. A number of these so-called Successors managed to carve out considerable territorial niches—kingdoms or mini-empires of their own. Ptolemy, a Macedonian aristocrat who had served on Alexander's general staff, ended up in charge of Egypt.

At first, Ptolemy refrained from proclaiming himself king of Egypt. For a while he ruled the country in Alexander's name while struggling with the other Successors to gain still more territory. Eventually, Ptolemy added parts of Palestine and Asia Minor (what is now Turkey) and the large island of Cyprus to his new realm. In 304 B.C. he finally felt confident enough to call himself pharaoh. And in so doing he established a new Egyptian dynasty (family of rulers)—the Ptolemaic dynasty. Ptolemy and his son (Ptolemy II Philadelphus) further distinguished their realm by building the Museum, a research center that attracted the greatest scholars in the world, and the largest library in the known world (both institutions in Alexandria).

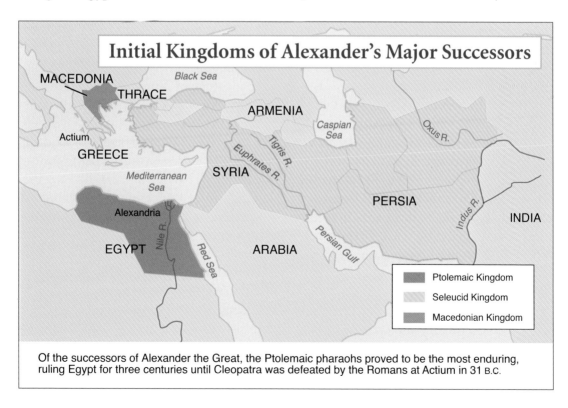

Of the successors of Alexander the Great, the Ptolemaic pharaohs proved to be the most enduring, ruling Egypt for three centuries until Cleopatra was defeated by the Romans at Actium in 31 B.C.

The Greek Upper Crust

Much of Cleopatra's later character, cultural attributes, style of rule, and relationship with the Egyptian people was shaped by the manner in which Ptolemy and his successors ruled Egypt. They did not institute democracy or some form of representative government, the most common political systems in the Greek lands. Instead, they administered Egypt as it had always been administered, as an absolute monarchy. For the average Egyptian, nothing changed with the coming of the new dynasty. Farmers continued to labor in the fields, producing the huge grain supplies for which the country was famous. And large numbers of these farmers carried on the tradition of working part-time on government building projects. The fact was that the changeover to a Greek ruling family had no significant psychological effect on a population that had grown used to being ruled by foreigners.

The rift between the rulers and their native subjects, which Cleopatra came to know well, was paralleled by one that existed between average Egyptians and the many Greeks who moved to Egypt during the years the Ptolemies ruled. At first it was almost like a gold rush in which young men from Greek cities eagerly sought to establish farms and businesses and raise families in what seemed to be a land of limitless opportunity. The Greek poet Theocritus immigrated to Alexandria, which had become a literary and cultural center, circa 270 B.C. A passage from one of his works describes the lure of Ptolemaic Egypt for Greeks at the time:

If you are ready to emigrate, Ptolemy is the freeman's paymaster, the best there is . . . a man of wit and taste . . . bestower of much upon many, no denier of favors, as befits a king. . . . If you have the courage . . . get you to Egypt.[8]

Encouraged by such tracts, as well as by abundant word of mouth, Greek merchants, soldiers, administrators, and artisans flocked to Egypt. But they did not intermarry or mix socially to any significant degree with the native Egyptians. Seeing the natives as culturally inferior, the Greeks, encouraged and supported by the Ptolemies, created a privileged class that treated non-Greeks as second-class citizens. The late, noted classical scholar Chester G. Starr summarized it this way: "Groups of relatively few Greeks constituted an upper crust much as did the English masters of Bombay, Singapore, or Hong Kong in the nineteenth century."[9]

A particularly central aspect of this classist society, one Cleopatra understood and specifically addressed during her reign, was the language barrier. During the Ptolemaic years, the Greek language became the lingua franca (universal tongue) of administration and business in Egypt. And most native Egyptians, who could neither speak, read, nor write it, had a difficult time getting ahead in life. Conversely, the Greeks who settled in Egypt made a conscious effort to resist absorbing Egyptian language and culture. All of the Ptolemaic rulers, except for the last—Cleopatra—refused to learn Egyptian; and this prejudice is reflected in

Alexandria's Famous Museum

The Museum, begun by Ptolemy I around 300 B.C. and maintained with pride by Cleopatra, was located on the north side of Alexandria's main avenue, adjoining the Ptolemaic palace complex. The institution was a research facility in which the greatest scholars of the ancient world lived, studied, experimented, and lectured. These scholars received financial subsidies from the Ptolemaic rulers (including Cleopatra), all of whom had a strong interest in the arts and learning.

Modern scholars have pieced together a picture of what the facility (which has not survived) looked like. Its outer façade featured a long, impressive colonnade. Inside, there was a large central hall with a high ceiling, a chamber in which scholars conferred and dined together. Most of the rest of the build-ing was divided into four sections, each devoted to the study of a different branch of knowledge (literature, mathematics, astronomy, and medicine). The Museum also had lecture halls, a library, a botanical garden, a small zoo (for housing research animals), and a theater.

Scholars conduct research in the Museum's library, which attracted some of the greatest scientists of ancient times.

the manner in which the Greek language evolved in the period. "In ordinary cultural contacts," scholar Naphtali Lewis points out,

handy words in the language of one group are readily adopted into the language of the other group. It would be difficult, therefore, to exaggerate the significance of the fact that . . . no native Egyptian word made its way into Greek usage in the thousand years that Greek endured as the language of Ptolemaic, Roman, and Byzantine

The World's Most Splendid City?

*Among the ancient writers who described Alexandria's unique and splendid layout was the first-century-*B.C.* Greek Diodorus Siculus. This excerpt is from volume 8 of his Library of History.*

[Alexander] laid out the site and traced the streets skillfully. . . . By selecting the right angle of the streets, Alexander made the city breathe with the etesian winds, so that as these blow across a great expanse of sea, they cool the air of the town, and so he provided its inhabitants with a moderate climate and good health. Alexander also laid out the walls so that they were at once exceedingly large and marvelously strong. . . . In shape, it [the city] is similar to a *chlamys* [military cloak], and it is approximately bisected by an avenue remarkable for its size and beauty. From gate to gate it runs a distance of [nearly five miles]; it is [one hundred feet] in width, and is bordered throughout its length with rich façades of houses and temples. . . . The city in general has grown so much in later times that many reckon it to be the first city of the civilized world, and it is certainly far ahead of all the rest in elegance and extent [size] and riches and luxury.

This modern reconstruction shows part of the palace sector of ancient Alexandria, where Cleopatra grew up in material splendor.

Egypt. This phenomenon can only mean that the Greek-speaking population actively resisted using or adopting Egyptian parlance.[10]

Living in Rome's Shadow

Not surprisingly, this aloofness and superior attitude on the part of the Greeks did not endear them to the native Egyptians. The Egyptian populace got used to, but never learned to like, the Greek rulers and upper classes. Meanwhile, the allure of Ptolemaic Egypt for outsiders steadily wore off at perhaps the same rate that the kingdom's power and prestige declined. Most of the Ptolemies, including Cleopatra's own father, were mediocre and unsympathetic rulers. They got themselves involved in wars with neighboring Greek states, conflicts that had indecisive results and ended up only needlessly draining the country's human and material resources.

At the same time, Rome rapidly became the strongest political power in the Mediterranean sphere. The Romans conquered most of the Greek world in the second century B.C. and imposed their influence and will on those Greek states they had not yet taken over. Thus, by the time Cleopatra was born, Egypt was still an independent nation; but it had become essentially a client (a state economically and militarily dependent on

This bust of Cleopatra's father as a young man is highly idealized.

another) of Rome. Ironically for the Greeks who dwelled in Egypt, the Romans looked on both Egyptians and Greeks there as inferiors. And the last Ptolemies had no choice but to try to impress and seek favors from the leading Romans of the day.

Living in Rome's shadow was therefore the political reality faced by Cleopatra's

Cleopatra stops to rest along the Nile with two attendants in a nineteenth-century painting that captures her luxurious lifestyle.

father, Ptolemy XII, popularly known as Auletes, "the Piper," because of his skill as a flute player. (The identity of Cleopatra's mother is unclear. Most scholars think she was Auletes' sister, Cleopatra V Tryphaina. For political expediency, the Ptolemies adopted the Egyptian custom of having royal siblings marry.) Auletes was an incompetent ruler. He mismanaged the treasury, which caused the country's already declining economic conditions to worsen. He also debased the coinage, reducing the silver content of coins to one-third. This made food prices and other aspects of the cost of living rise. In addition, Auletes tried to make up for these mistakes by levying heavy new taxes, an unwise move that drove most Egyptians to the brink of rebellion by 59 B.C., the year in which Cleopatra turned ten.

Growing Up in Splendor

It is probable that the young princess and her royal siblings (three sisters and two brothers) were well insulated from these troubles, at least when they were very young. Inside the palace and its extensive grounds, the young royals enjoyed comfortable, carefree lives. As scholar Michael

Foss describes it, Cleopatra "had within reach every luxury, every refinement known to the ancient world." Growing up in the wealthy Ptolemaic court,

> her health and physical well-being would have been in the hands of the best Alexandrian doctors. There were no better doctors [at the time in the world]. Her tutors would have come from the community of scholars living almost in the shade of the palace, in the halls of the Museum and the Library.[11]

In addition, Cleopatra grew up wearing the finest clothes available, eating the best native and imported foods, and enjoyed the attentions of numerous servants who catered to her every need.

Cleopatra's character, or at least her education and the amazing worldliness she would display as an adult ruler, was also shaped in some degree by what lay outside the palace walls. Alexandria was by this time one of the three largest cities in the known world (along with Rome, Italy, and Antioch, Syria). Alexandria was also a supremely cosmopolitan city. It had its native Egyptian neighborhoods, but it also featured large Greek sections and a Jewish quarter. And sailors, merchants, and tourists from Ethiopia, Syria, Arabia, and numerous other lands regularly visited. This melting pot of languages and cultures seems to have made a strong impression on the young Cleopatra. Plutarch later reported that she was fluent in Syriac, Arabic, and Hebrew as well as Greek and Egyptian.

The Alexandria of Cleopatra's youth was also a physically imposing place filled with grand avenues, architectural wonders, excellent shopping districts, and modern conveniences. Both Pliny the Elder and the Greek geographer Strabo said that the city, as seen from above, resembled a very big chlamys (military cloak). Strabo added the following:

> The city as a whole is intersected by streets practicable for horse-riding and chariot-driving . . . and contains most beautiful public precincts . . . [for] each of the kings, from love of splendor, was wont to add some adornment to the public monuments . . . so that now, to quote the words of the poet, "there is building on building." . . . The city is [also] full of dedications and shrines. Finest of all is the gymnasium, the colonnades in the center of which are more than a stade [600 feet] in length, and also the Courts of Justice. . . . There is also the Paneion [temple of the woodland god Pan], an artificial circular mound in the shape of a fir-cone, resembling a rocky hill, with a spiral path to the summit; and from the top the whole city can be seen spread out beneath on all sides.[12]

Among the other wonders one could see in this panorama were the Museum and the Great Library, which adjoined the massive Ptolemaic palaces. There were also two harbors. One—the eastern, or Great Harbor—was roughly circular with a diameter of about a mile and a half. It featured a series of wide, well-maintained docks and ship sheds. These served as the home base for the Ptolemaic royal war fleets as well as large royal pleasure barges like the one on which Cleopatra would later wine and dine Mark Antony. Most imposing of all was Alexandria's great lighthouse. It stood on the small Pharos Island, which formed the northern border of one harbor. Erected by the early Ptolemies, the structure was hundreds of feet tall, and the light it projected (via a fire reflected by large mirrors) could be seen by sailors far out at sea.

Auletes' Troubles

When Cleopatra and her siblings were very young, the magnificent and urbane Alexandria may have seemed like a giant and fantastic playground. But for their father during these same years, having a splendid capital did not lessen the seriousness of the difficulties he faced as a ruler. With economic conditions in Egypt worsening and his subjects getting increasingly restless and angry over the high taxes he imposed, in 58 B.C. (when Cleopatra was about eleven) Auletes turned to the only remedy he could think of. It was one that several of his predecessors had chosen as well. Namely, he tried to get the backing of one or more of the most powerful and influential Romans of the day. Auletes hoped that they would intercede on his behalf with the Roman Senate. If the senators proclaimed him a "friend and ally" of Rome, he reasoned, he would become more respected and feared at home and his troubles would diminish.

At the time that Auletes set his plan in motion, the three leading Roman figures were the politician Julius Caesar, the military general Gnaeus Pompeius (called "Pompey" for short), and the real estate tycoon Marcus Crassus, the richest man in Rome. It turned out that Caesar was then short of cash. So he willingly took a bribe in return for submitting a resolution to the Senate (of which he was a member) that named Auletes Rome's friend and ally. The bribe amounted to six thousand talents, equivalent to tens of millions of dollars in today's money.

The relieved but ultimately short-sighted Auletes returned to Egypt to find that his mission had been largely a waste of time. First, the huge sum he had given Caesar had practically emptied the treasury, and the only way to replenish it was to impose still more burdensome taxes on the Egyptian people. This and other political blunders he made soon afterward were viewed by them "as clear evidence that as a king he was a total failure,"[13] as scholar Ernle Bradford puts it.

With Auletes' public approval at an all-time low, a rebellion broke out and he was forced to flee the country. The desperate pharaoh once more saw no other choice than to appeal to the Romans for help. His need of aid became even greater once he learned that, in his absence, his daughter Cleopatra Tryphaina (sister of Cleopatra VII and namesake of their mother) had snatched the throne. More stunning news came only a few weeks later: The young usurper had been murdered and another of Auletes' daughters, Berenice, had seized power.

The true appearance of Cleopatra's throne room is unknown. This engraving by an early modern artist attempts to reconstruct it.

Cleopatra Inherits the Throne

When Auletes reached Rome, he once more turned to money as a means of solving his problems. This time he had no money for bribes, however. So he floated promissory notes that guaranteed he would later pay a huge sum to the Roman notable who funded a military expedition and reinstated him in Egypt. Both Pompey and Crassus almost took this bait. But perhaps to their surprise, the Roman governor of Syria, Aulus Gabinius, accepted the job first. Gabinius assembled his troops, marched them to Egypt, and restored Auletes to his throne. (The pharaoh summarily executed Berenice and her leading supporters.)

In the end, however, all of Auletes' strenuous efforts were in vain. A few years later, in 51 B.C., he died, miserable and hated by nearly everyone, both inside and outside the palace. It is unknown how Cleopatra, then about eighteen, felt about her father, but there is no doubt that his death worked to her benefit. With her two older sisters dead, she was next in line for the throne.

And Auletes' will instructed that she and her ten-year-old brother, Ptolemy XIII, were to rule the realm jointly.

The eager young woman soon found that maintaining her authority was not going to be easy. A rivalry with her brother almost immediately began, leading to tensions and threats. Young Ptolemy's regent (adult adviser and protector), Pothinus, the most powerful figure in the royal court, disliked Cleopatra. Seeking to make the boy sole ruler, Pothinus intrigued behind the queen's back, discrediting her with the courtiers and army generals.

The exact nature of these schemes is unknown, but they clearly worked. In September 49 B.C. Cleopatra felt compelled to flee the capital, and she ended up taking refuge in Syria. There, she began raising an army with which she hoped to unseat her brother and reclaim the throne. At the time she had no way of knowing that powerful currents in the larger tide of Roman political affairs would soon sweep her into a destiny that would earn her eternal renown.

◆ Chapter Two

Lover and Ally: Cleopatra and Julius Caesar

In 48 B.C., while the deposed young Egyptian queen, Cleopatra, did her best to raise an army in Syria, fate was working in her favor in another sector of the Mediterranean world. At Pharsalus in Greece, the armies of Caesar and Pompey came to death grips. A little more than a decade before, Caesar, Pompey, and the other major Roman power broker, Crassus, had formed an informal alliance, the so-called First Triumvirate ("group of three"). Pooling their considerable resources, they had exerted undue influence over the Roman government. But in time this powerful partnership had fallen apart. Crassus had been killed in an unsuccessful military venture in the Near East, and in 49 Caesar and Pompey had faced off in a bloody civil war that had rocked the Roman realm.

After Caesar decisively defeated Pompey at Pharsalus, the beaten Pompey chose Egypt as a refuge. It was this fact that forever changed Cleopatra's fortunes. Pompey may have reasoned that his former business meet-

ings with Ptolemy XII Auletes made him a sort of friend of the royal family. At any rate, Egypt was rich in grain and ships and promising as a place to raise a new army to oppose Caesar. But would there be enough time for Pompey to regroup before Caesar came to Egypt in pursuit of his enemy? As it happened, this question became moot when Pompey met an unexpected demise and Cleopatra shrewdly took full advantage of the bizarre political situation that ensued.

Pompey and Caesar Arrive in Egypt

After his flight from Greece, Pompey's small flotilla of ships arrived off Egypt's northern shore near the spot where young King Ptolemy's army had gathered to confront the one that Cleopatra had raised. Caesar himself later described the situation in one of his famous journals, the *Commentary on the Civil Wars:*

As it happened, King Ptolemy, who was only a boy, was there at the head of a large force, at war with his sister Cleopatra, whom he had ejected from the kingdom a few months beforehand. . . . And Cleopatra's [military] camp was no great distance from his. Pompey sent him a request that for the sake of his ties of friendship and hospitality . . . he be given refuge at Alexandria and protected in his misfortune by the king's power.[14]

Caesar went on to speculate that perhaps Ptolemy and his advisers feared that Pompey might try to seize control of Alexandria. Or maybe they figured it was safer for them to side with the winner, rather than the loser, of the Roman civil war. Whatever their motives, according to Appian, these high-placed Egyptians "arranged a council to discuss what to do about Pompey," and one of them proposed that they should "entrap and kill" him in hopes of impressing and pleasing Caesar. Pothinus and Ptolemy approved of the plan, and as Pompey approached the Egyptian shore, his "head was cut off" by assassins "and someone buried the rest of the body on the shore."[15]

Just four days later Caesar arrived in Egypt at the head of a small contingent of troops. He was not only surprised to discover that Pompey had been murdered, but he was also disgusted and outraged when presented with his former partner's severed head. This part of Ptolemy's and Pothinus's scheme had clearly backfired. And there was more bad news for them. Caesar suddenly and firmly demanded that the Egyptian leaders pay him a large sum of money. (This was the unpaid portion of the huge loans Auletes had taken out in 58 and 57 B.C. with a wealthy Roman financier named Rabirius. Caesar had promised Rabirius that he would collect the money while he was in Egypt, almost certainly in exchange for a hefty commission.)

This eighteenth-century Italian statue of Julius Caesar was based on ancient models.

A sixteenth-century Italian painting depicts Julius Caesar (center, sitting below the statue) visiting Egypt.

Pothinus not only tried to avoid paying the money, but also treated Caesar with considerable disrespect while the famous general was staying at the palace. According to Plutarch:

Even openly Pothinus made himself intolerable, belittling and insulting Caesar both in his words and his actions. For instance, the soldiers [Roman officers accompanying Caesar] were given rations of the oldest and worst possible grain, and Pothi-nus told them that they must put up with it and learn to like it, since they were eating food that did not belong to them. And at official dinners he gave orders that wooden and earthenware dishes should be used, on the pretext that Caesar had taken all the gold and silver in payment of a debt. The father of the present king did in fact owe Caesar [actually Rabirius] 17 ½ million drachmas . . . and Caesar now demanded 10 million for the support of his army. Pothinus suggested that for the time being [Caesar] should go away and attend to more important matters, promising that later on they would be delighted to pay the money.[16]

Not surprisingly, Caesar was not about to accept this dodge and made it plain that he would stay in Alexandria as long as it took to collect the debt.

Cleopatra Makes Her Move

In the meantime, Caesar and Cleopatra were drawn together because of their mutual distrust and opposition to Ptolemy and Pothinus. Plutarch claims that Caesar "secretly sent for Cleopatra from the country."[17] Evidently he felt that she might be a valuable ally in the present standoff with her enemies at court. At the same time, it is reasonable to assume that she was already planning to meet with Caesar and win him over to her cause.

In any case, the ambitious young woman acted boldly. Their first meeting, as recorded by Plutarch in one of the most famous passages in ancient literature, smacks of fable at first glance. However, Plutarch was a serious writer who was not given to repeating hearsay without labeling it as such. Also, he had the advantage of some inside sources; in one case, his grandfather had been friends with an Alexandrian doctor who had been at Cleopatra's court. That doctor, who had also known Antony's son quite well, passed on many juicy details about the Egyptian queen and her escapades. "Taking only one of her friends with her (Apollodorus the Sicilian)," Plutarch writes, Cleopatra

embarked in a small boat and landed at the palace when it was already getting dark. Since there seemed to be no other way of getting in, she stretched herself out at full length inside a sleeping bag, and Apollodorus, after tying up the bag, carried it indoors to Caesar. This little trick of Cleopatra's, which showed her provocative impudence, is said to have been the first thing about her which captivated Caesar, and as he grew to know her better he was overcome by her charm.[18]

If Cleopatra's audaciousness and personal charm drew Caesar to her, what qualities drew the young woman to this older man? At the time, after all, she was twenty-one and he was fifty-two. On the one hand, political considerations were certainly in play. Caesar was the most powerful man in the world, and Cleopatra badly needed his support to oppose her brother and regain the throne. Yet some surviving evidence suggests that real bonds of mutual admiration developed between the Roman general and the Egyptian princess. Michael Foss provides this useful sketch of those talents and character traits of Caesar's that could not have failed to impress a young woman who respected leaders as bold, crafty, and ruthless as she was:

Soldier, scholar, writer, administrator, man of business, politician, visionary

One of several modern depictions of Cleopatra's famous first meeting with Caesar (sitting at the desk) after smuggling herself into the palace.

statesman, he encompassed whatever he set his hand to. He combined learning with sharp, swift judgment in practical affairs. . . . He was bold in decision, brave in battle, stoical and uncomplaining about hardship, and he was famously popular with his troops. . . . He was also vain, ruthless, calculating . . . and always driven by his own ambition. . . . His friends felt the warm sun of a great and power-ful personality; his enemies courted a sudden death.[19]

Caesar and Cleopatra were so taken with each other, in fact, that they immediately became lovers as well as political allies. He told the startled Ptolemy and Pothinus that he was backing her claims to the throne. They must honor the terms of Auletes' will, Caesar insisted, and allow Cleopatra to rule jointly with Ptolemy.

Caesar and Cleopatra Are Besieged

Taken off guard by Cleopatra's presence in the palace and her sudden alliance with Caesar, Ptolemy and Pothinus tentatively agreed to do as Caesar demanded. But they had no intention of keeping their word. Pothinus secretly sent orders to the Egyptian general Achillas to bring his army and surround the palace. These forces "were not to be despised," Caesar later admitted. Achillas "had 20,000 men under arms," while in contrast, my forces were much too small for me to place any confidence in them if I had to fight outside the city. The only course open to me was to remain in my position in the town and find out Achillas's intentions. None the less, I ordered all my men to stay under arms.[20]

The ensuing situation was strange to say the least. On the one hand, Caesar and Cleopatra were trapped in the royal palace complex. "Achillas occupied Alexandria," Caesar recalled, "except for the part of the town which I held [the section occupied

Caesar, who has been romanticized in art as much as Cleopatra, holds the world in the palm of his hand as he parades in triumph on horseback.

With his first assault he attempted to break into my quarters, but I had my [men] spread about the streets and withstood the assault. At the same time there was fighting by the harbor, and that brought by far the most serious struggle. Fighting was taking place . . . over a considerable number of streets, and simultaneously the enemy was trying with a large body of men to gain control of the [Roman] warships. . . . If the enemy got possession of them, they would have wrested the fleet from me, and would have the port and the open sea entirely under their control. . . . [So] I burned all these ships.[22]

by the royal palaces, lying east of the great harbor], with his soldiers."[21] On the other hand, Ptolemy and Pothinus were trapped there as well because Caesar kept them under guard. As the conflict that the Romans came to call the Alexandrian War erupted, the opposing leaders coexisted in the palace, an uncomfortable situation that was destined to last for almost two months.

Cleopatra's and Caesar's position was dangerous as well as uncomfortable. Achillas repeatedly ordered assaults on Caesar's guards outside the palace and even tried to enter the royal complex. Caesar later wrote:

Cleopatra and her Roman mentor found themselves in another sticky situation when her sister, Arsinoe (ar-SIN-oh-eh), snuck out of the palace, joined Achillas, and proclaimed herself sole ruler of Egypt. Soon, however, Arsinoe turned on Achillas and executed him. She put her own adviser in charge of the war, and he cut off the flow of fresh water into the palace. But they had seriously underestimated their opponent, for Caesar ordered his men to dig wells near the harbor beach. According to an anonymous ancient chronicle of the conflict, "With every man roused to throw himself into the work, a copious

Caesar Describes the Opposing Army

In this excerpt from his journal about the civil war Caesar gave a thumbnail sketch of the Egyptian army that besieged him and Cleopatra.

Achillas [the Egyptian commander] was accompanied by forces of a sort not to be despised, either in quantity and type of troops or in military experience. He had 20,000 men under arms. These consisted of Gabinius's soldiers [the Roman troops who had earlier put Cleopatra's father back on his throne and afterward stayed in Egypt in service to the local government], who had by now become habituated to the ill-disciplined ways of Alexandrian life and had unlearned the good name and orderly conduct of Romans. . . . In addition to these there were men gathered from among the pirates and brigands of Syria . . . and adjoining regions. Also, many exiles and men condemned to loss of citizen rights had collected here. . . . There were in addition two thousand cavalry.

In this sixteenth-century painting, Caesar writes his commentaries on the civil war.

This Renaissance painting of Caesar shows the Roman leading Cleopatra to her throne. The artist has dressed his subjects in the clothing styles of his own day.

[abundant] supply of fresh water was discovered in a single night."[23]

Back on the Throne

Indeed, despite the larger size of their army, Arsinoe, Ptolemy, and Pothinus were well out of their league in their fight with Caesar. First, the Roman general had Pothinus killed. Then reinforcements Caesar had sent for earlier arrived, and with these he easily defeated the Egyptian army in a pitched battle. Ptolemy fled and drowned when his boat became overloaded with

other fleeing Egyptians and sank. As for Arsinoe, Caesar captured her and held her in chains in anticipation of forcing her to march in his upcoming triumph (victory parade).

Cleopatra now benefited handsomely from the victory of her lover and ally. He reinstated her as Egypt's queen in a splendid ceremony. He also saw to it that Cleopatra married her surviving brother, twelve-year-old Ptolemy XIV, a wise political move designed to show the Egyptians that Rome respected their traditions. The marriage posed no threat to Cleopatra's

Several disgruntled senators stab Caesar to death at the base of a statue of his political opponent, Pompey, in this nineteenth-century painting.

authority. Unlike Ptolemy XIII, the new king had no powerful regent other than the queen herself, who was now in effect sole ruler of Egypt.

Cleopatra seems to have been delighted when she learned that Caesar planned to stay in Egypt for a while. To show her appreciation for his efforts on her behalf, she took him on a cruise "up" the Nile. (Actually, they traveled southward since in ancient times the region of the Nile Delta was called Lower Egypt and the areas farther south were called Upper Egypt.) Appian says that Caesar "made a voyage on the Nile to look at the country with a flotilla of 400 ships in the company of Cleopatra,

and enjoyed himself with her in other ways as well." [24] If the number of ships Appian cites is not an exaggeration, most were not warships. Rather, the bulk of the armada probably consisted of small sloops and barges, many carrying the numerous servants and wide range of supplies and creature comforts the queen needed to entertain properly.

After a few months Caesar was obliged to end his frivolities with his new ally and return to more pressing matters, namely finishing the war he had been engaged in before arriving in Egypt. He left Alexandria early in 47 B.C. to put down a rebellion in Asia Minor. The words he and

Cleopatra exchanged at his departure will never be known. What seems certain is that, as both were realists, they appreciated that their political alliance took precedence over any personal feelings they had for each other. Also, they could take solace in the knowledge that they were sure to meet again. As Caesar climbed aboard his ship, it is likely that he was aware that Cleopatra was pregnant with his child.

Caesar's Blood

The exact time of the baby's birth is unknown. But Cleopatra definitely took the child with her to Rome a little more than a year later, following Caesar's victories over his last rivals. During the period of his triumphs (several, each celebrating one of a long string of military successes), he arranged for her to stay in a magnificent villa located on the opposite side of the Tiber River from the capital. According to the second-century Roman historian Suetonius, Caesar lavished "high titles and rich presents" on her, and "even allowed her to call the son whom she had borne him by his own name." This informal name was Caesarion, although his Egyptian title was Ptolemy XV Caesar. Suetonius also said that "the boy closely resembled Caesar in features as well as in gait [carriage]." [25]

In later years Cleopatra's enemies in Rome tried to erase the memory of her presence there. But they were not totally successful. After Cleopatra left the city, the great Roman senator and orator Marcus Tullius Cicero wrote a letter that briefly described some of her activities in Rome.

(This letter, in fact, is the only surviving ancient document that does so.) Evidently, at some earlier social gathering Cleopatra had promised Cicero that her servant would deliver him some books (or some other literary materials) as gifts. But Cicero never received them and felt slighted. "I dislike Her Majesty," he wrote in the letter. "The arrogance of the queen herself when she was living on the estate across the Tiber makes my blood boil to recall. So I want nothing to do with them [the queen and her associates]." [26]

Cicero was not overly fond of Caesar either, as the two men had been political enemies for many years. Still, the aging senator was fairly shocked when some of his colleagues stabbed Caesar to death in the Senate House on March 15, 44 B.C. (Among other things, they were outraged that he had recently declared himself dictator for life.) For Cleopatra, the assassination was a tragedy and a dilemma of the first order. Her lover and benefactor, who had also been the father of her son, was dead and she was left to fend for herself far from home. Not surprisingly, she wasted little time in gathering her belongings and returning to Egypt. She and Caesarion arrived in Alexandria in July.

Cleopatra was not naive enough to think that her involvement in Roman power politics was over. After all, the blood of the mighty Caesar flowed through her son's veins. And she sat on the throne of one of the world's richest countries. Sooner or later, she likely reasoned, some prominent Roman would try to exploit one or both of these valuable assets.

Chapter Three

LOVER AND ALLY AGAIN: CLEOPATRA AND MARK ANTONY

History has shown that Cleopatra was a keen and shrewd political observer and player. During the two years following Julius Caesar's assassination, she was mostly an observer, which turned out to be a wise approach. From her vantage in Alexandria, she witnessed the Roman world convulse in a state of political and military upheaval. Caesar had been the most powerful person who had ever lived, and his death had left behind a vacuum of enormous proportions. Three ambitious men quickly stepped forward in hopes of filling this power vacuum: Mark Antony, who had been one of Caesar's top military lieutenants; Octavian, Caesar's eighteen-year-old adopted son; and Marcus Lepidus, a popular general who had also served with distinction under Caesar.

As Cleopatra watched quietly, but with great interest, in 43 B.C. these three men formed a second political triumvirate. Their stated goal was to "restore order" to the Roman realm. But the principal items on

their real agenda were to entrench their own power as firmly as possible and to divide up the empire among themselves. They knew that to accomplish these aims it would be necessary to confront and eliminate two major factions that opposed them. One faction was made up of their political enemies in Rome, mainly aging champions of the Republic and its traditional ideals. In a terrifying political purge, the triumvirs murdered or otherwise silenced these men, including the great orator Cicero, who was beheaded by Antony's henchmen.

The second group of opponents that stood in the triumvirs' way consisted of the surviving members of the conspiracy against Caesar. Their ringleaders, Brutus and Cassius, wanted to restore the senatorial prestige that had recently declined under Caesar and other military strongmen. To this end, the former conspirators were in Greece raising troops to fight the triumvirs. With one of the biggest military showdowns in Mediterranean history looming, Cassius sent requests for soldiers, ships, and economic aid to rulers throughout the Near East, including Cleopatra.

In this way, the Egyptian queen eventually found herself compelled to take sides in a conflict that would be fought far beyond her nation's borders. For Cleopatra, backing the conspirators who had killed her lover and ally Caesar was out of the question. Accordingly, she sent word to Cassius that ongoing bouts of famine and disease in her land made it impossible for her to help him. In the meantime, she assembled a fleet of ships and sailed north, intending to aid the triumvirs. At this point Cleopatra hardly knew Antony and did not know Octavian at all. And there was every indication that they were ambitious, selfish individuals who could not be totally trusted. But at least they had been backers of Caesar.

As it happened, however, nature intervened and kept Cleopatra from taking part in the ensuing battle for world dominance. A large storm wrecked many of her ships, and she was forced to return to Alexandria. A mere observer once more, she had no choice for the moment but to wait and see which side won the ongoing civil war. At the time she could not have foreseen that the victor would become an ally and lover even more devoted to her than Caesar had been.

A portrait bust of Marcus Agrippa, a close friend and military adviser of Caesar's adopted son, Octavian.

The Territorial Pie

In fact, Cleopatra did not have to wait long to discover the identity of the winner of the war. Agents she had sent to Greece kept her posted as events there speedily unfolded. By the fall of 42 B.C., Brutus and Cassius had gathered more than eighty thousand troops, who assembled on the plain

One of several early modern paintings depicting a famous scene described by Plutarch— the arrival of Cleopatra's pleasure barge at Tarsus.

of Philippi in northern Greece to fight the oncoming forces of Antony and Octavian. Two pitched battles took place, separated by an interval of three weeks. Appian later dramatically described the ugly mood on the battlefield in the minutes before the decisive second encounter began:

> At the present moment they [the soldiers] had not the slightest recollection that they were all Romans, and they issued threats against each other as though they were natural enemies by race. Thus, their immediate fury overwhelmed their powers of reasoning and their nature, and both sides alike prophesied that that day and that

battle would decide the entire fate of Rome. And decided it was.[27]

The ensuing struggle was long and bloody. In the end, Antony's and Octavian's forces were victorious, and their opponents were humiliated and psychologically devastated. Their cause forever lost, Brutus and Cassius committed suicide, and with them died the last credible chance of restoring the Roman Republic.

Cleopatra also listened with interest as her agents described the actions of the triumvirs in the weeks and months following their great victory. As she had fully expected they would, the three men proceeded to divide up the Roman world among themselves. Octavian got Spain and the large island of Sardinia (off Italy's western coast), and Lepidus got the Roman provinces of North Africa. In contrast, Antony, who had been the principal general at Philippi and who was seen as the dominant partner in the triumvirate, received the best parts of the territorial pie. He became master of the "East," the region consisting of the Roman provinces in Greece, Asia Minor, and the Near East. This gave him huge authority and influence over a number of weak independent eastern kingdoms, including Cleopatra's Egypt.

In this way, the outcome of the civil war created a situation in which Cleopatra and Antony were bound sooner or later to meet and interact. Actually, they had met briefly twice before. The first time was in 57 B.C., when she was twelve and he was a young officer in the Roman army that had put her father back on his stolen throne. They had also briefly exchanged words in Rome shortly before Caesar's assassination, in 44, when Antony was still Caesar's trusted lieutenant.

Their third encounter was to prove a great deal more fateful. Now in charge of the East, Antony, a hard-drinking, no-nonsense soldier, saw an opportunity to gain military prestige and glory that might rival that of his former mentor, Caesar. Rome still viewed the Parthians, who had revived the old Persian Empire (in what are now Iran and Iraq), as enemies. And Antony was confident he could invade and defeat Parthia and bring its lands into the Roman fold. To do so, however, he needed a lot of ships, troops, grain, and, above all, money. The lands of the eastern Mediterranean all

The Murder of Cicero

In his Life of Cicero *(translated by Rex Warner in* Fall of the Roman Republic*), Plutarch recorded how Antony's henchmen caught up with the Republic's last great defender:*

The murderers had arrived [at Cicero's villa]. These were the centurion Herennius and Popillius, an officer of the army. . . . They had their helpers with them. They found the doors shut and broke them down; but Cicero was not to be seen and the people in the house said that they did not know where he was. Then . . . a young man. . . told the officer that the litter [on which Cicero was riding] was being carried down to the sea by a path that was under the cover of the trees. The officer took a few men with him and hurried round to the place where the path came out of the woods, and Herennius went running down the path. Cicero heard him coming and ordered his servants to set the litter down where they were. He himself, in that characteristic posture of his, with his chin resting on his left hand, looked steadfastly at his murderers. He was all covered in dust; his hair was long and disordered, and his face was pinched and wasted with his anxieties—so that most of those who stood by covered their faces while Herennius was killing him. His throat was cut as he stretched his neck out from the litter.

Venus Comes to Bacchus

Cleopatra was hardly surprised, therefore, when in the late summer of 41 B.C. Antony summoned her to his headquarters at Tarsus (in Cilicia in southern Asia Minor). Plutarch described her preparations for the meeting. It must be kept in mind that he, like most other Greco-Roman writers of those times, accepted Roman propaganda that pictured Cleopatra as a scheming, power-hungry enchantress who purposely set out to seduce and control the most powerful Roman men of the day. (This slanted version of characters and events did more than treat the Egyptian queen unfairly and distort history. It also portrayed Caesar, Antony, and other Roman notables as naive, easily manipulated individuals lacking strength and self-control; clearly, if they had actually been that weak and gullible, they could not have achieved such powerful positions.) Cleopatra "had already seen for herself the power of her beauty to enchant Julius Caesar," Plutarch writes,

> and she expected to conquer Antony even more easily. For Caesar . . . had known her when she was still a young girl with no experience of the world, but she was to meet Antony at the age when a woman's beauty is at its most superb and her mind at its most mature. [She was then about twenty-eight.] She therefore provided herself with a lavish supply of gifts, money,

and ornaments as her exalted position and the prosperity of her kingdom made it appropriate to take, but she relied above all upon her physical presence and the spell and enchantment which it could create.[28]

Plutarch went on to describe her memorable entrance into the harbor at Tarsus, a scene that would later be re-created in countless books, paintings, and movies:

> She came sailing up the river Cydnus in a barge with a stern of gold, its purple sails billowing in the wind, while her rowers caressed the water with oars of silver which dipped in time to the music of the flute, accompanied by pipes and lutes. Cleopatra herself reclined beneath a canopy of gold cloth, dressed as Venus [Roman goddess of love] . . . while on either side . . . stood boys costumed as Cupids, who cooled her with fans. Instead of a crew, her barge was lined with the most beautiful of her waiting-women attired as [minor goddesses], some at the rudders, other at the . . . sails, and all the while an indescribably rich perfume . . . was wafted from the vessel to the river-banks. Great multitudes [of local people] accompanied this royal progress, some of them following the queen on both sides of the river from its very mouth, while others hurried down from the city of Tarsus to gaze at the sight. . . . The word spread on every side that Venus had come to revel with Bacchus [or

Another modern rendition of Cleopatra's arrival at Tarsus shows Antony greeting her on the riverbank.

Dionysus, a reference to Antony's identification of himself with this popular fertility god] for the happiness of Asia.[29]

After Cleopatra had made her grand entrance, Antony sent her an invitation to dinner. But she insisted that he dine with her instead. "He found the preparations made to receive him magnificent beyond words," Plutarch writes. Antony was particularly impressed by the large number of oil lamps and braziers (metal receptacles that burned charcoal or wood) scattered throughout the interior of the queen's barge. These "created as brilliant a spectacle as can ever have been devised to delight the eye."[30]

The next day it was Antony's turn to throw a banquet. He apologized to Cleopatra for not being able to match the splendor of her party and even poked fun at how meager his own gathering was in comparison. It appears that Antony had a good sense of humor, even if it was, as Plutarch said, "broad and gross and belonged to the soldier rather than the courtier." Nevertheless, the Egyptian queen found his simple, straightforward manner refreshing. Or at least she took it in her stride and "adopted the same manner towards him." This incident affords a rare glimpse of Cleopatra's considerable social graces and charms, which allowed her to hold her own in conversations and meetings with educated, accomplished men, a rarity among women in those days. Here, once again, Plutarch was likely drawing on the recollections of his grandfather's friend, who had known people who had directly interacted with Antony and Cleopatra. "The charm of her presence was irresistible," the Greek biographer continues,

> and there was an attraction in her person and her talk, together with a peculiar force of character which pervaded her every word and action. . . . It was a delight merely to hear the sound of her voice, with which, like an instrument of many strings, she could pass [effortlessly] from one language to another.[31]

Winter in Alexandria

Eventually, after they had gotten to know each other, Cleopatra and Antony got down to business. He bluntly told her that he required money, grain, and other sorts of aid to help make his Parthian campaign a success. But if he thought that the queen was going to provide him these things simply out of fear or respect for a powerful Roman triumvir, he was sorely mistaken. Cleopatra was as blunt and fearless as he was and drove a hard bargain. She said she was willing to back his Parthian adventure, but for a price. First, he must agree to protect her against her enemies, whether domestic or foreign, something he clearly had the military power and reputation to accomplish.

Antony agreed to this condition. And the wily Cleopatra immediately gave him a test that would determine whether his word was good. After her humiliating march in chains in Caesar's triumph a few years before, the queen's sister, Arsinoe, had been released. She had taken refuge in a temple in Ephesus (in Asia Minor), where she still made trouble for Cleopatra by claiming to be the rightful ruler of Egypt. Cleopatra wanted this thorn in her side removed, and Antony wasted no time in removing it. As the stalwart Cicero had two years before, Arsinoe soon received a fateful visit from Antony's executioners.

Antony now had a deal that gave him the valuable Egyptian aid he had sought. But his march into Parthia was not scheduled to begin until the following spring. So he cheerfully accepted Cleopatra's invitation to spend the winter with her in Alexandria. There, despite the fact that Antony was a married man, the two cavorted for months, enjoying extravagant feasts and parties almost on a daily basis. Some idea of the splendor of these gatherings comes from a story told by Plutarch's grandfather's physician friend. He had "made the acquaintance of one of the royal cooks," Plutarch writes, and the cook invited him

> to come and see the lavish preparations which were made for a royal dinner [in Cleopatra's palace]. [The doctor] was introduced into the kitchens of the palace, and, after he had seen the enormous abundance of provisions and watched eight wild boars being roasted, he expressed his astonishment at the size of the company for which this vast hospitality was intended. The cook

Cleopatra's Pearls

Many stories about Cleopatra have been told over the centuries, some more believable than others. One unlikely account comes from the writings of the esteemed Roman scholar Pliny the Elder. In his Natural History *(translated by John F. Healy) Pliny claims that Cleopatra once dissolved pearls in vinegar and drank them.*

Two specimen pearls were the largest of all time. Cleopatra . . . owned both. . . . Headstrong woman that she was . . . Cleopatra ordered [her] servants [to] set before her only a single vessel of vinegar, the acidity of which can dissolve pearls. [In reality, it cannot.] . . . Antony waited breathlessly to see what on earth she was going to do. Cleopatra took off one earring, dropped the pearl in the vinegar and, when it had dissolved, swallowed it. . . . The story is told that when Cleopatra . . . was [later] captured, the second pearl was cut in two, so that half . . . might adorn each ear of the statue of Venus in the Pantheon in Rome.

A seventeenth-century painting depicts Cleopatra dissolving a pearl in vinegar, as reported by Pliny.

laughed aloud and explained that this was not a large party, [but] only about a dozen people, but that everything must be cooked and served to perfection. . . . [Also] it might be that Antony would call for a meal as soon as the guests had arrived, or a little later he might postpone it and call for a cup of wine, or become absorbed in some conversation. "So we never prepare one

Cleopatra and Antony dine in this eighteenth-century Italian painting. She is about to dip the pearl in the vinegar.

supper," [the cook] explained, "but a whole number of them, as we never know the exact moment when they will be sent for."[32]

In addition to feasts and drinking parties, Cleopatra and Antony engaged in numerous other leisure activities during his stay in the capital. Like many soldiers, he enjoyed earthy pastimes, including playing dice and hunting. And he was delighted when the young queen joined him in these activities. The two also took part in some rather juvenile and somewhat risky role-playing games in which he disguised himself as a slave and she dressed up as a maid-servant. They went out into the streets, and Antony would poke his head into people's windows and call them names, after which he and she would run away. At times, according to ancient sources, they were pursued and occasionally Antony suffered minor beatings; but apparently they considered this all part of the fun.

Other ancient accounts of Cleopatra and Antony's leisure exploits seem to support the idea that they came truly and thoroughly to enjoy each other's company. One of the most charming of these stories describes one of their fishing trips:

[Antony] had no luck with his line . . . so he ordered some fishermen to dive down and secretly to fasten on his hook a number of fish they had already caught. Then he proceeded to pull up his line. . . . But the queen discovered the trick. She pretended to admire his success, but . . . [the next day] when Antony had let down his line Cleopatra ordered one of her own servants to swim immediately to his hook and fix onto it a salted fish from the Black Sea. Antony, believing he had made a catch, pulled up his line, whereupon the whole company [of courtiers and servants] burst out laughing, and Cleopatra told him: "Emperor, you had better give up your [fishing] rod to us poor rulers of [Egypt]. Your sport is to hunt cities and kingdoms and continents." [33]

Antony's Departure

At the time, Cleopatra surely meant these words in an innocent way. But there was more truth and prophecy in them than she realized. Antony was indeed first and foremost a soldier as well as a triumvir with enormous powers and responsibilities in the wider world beyond Alexandria.

The reality of these facts hit home early in 40 B.C. when a messenger from Greece arrived in the Egyptian capital. The man brought news that Antony's wife, Fulvia, and his brother, Lucius, had led a rebellion against Octavian back in Italy. Their motive had been to eliminate the younger triumvir so that Antony could rule Octavian's portion of the realm along with his own. But the insurrection had failed. Lucius had been taken prisoner, and Fulvia had fled to Greece.

According to Plutarch, on hearing this news Antony was "like a man who had been roughly awoken after sleeping off a heavy [drunken stupor]." [34] As he hastily prepared to leave to meet his wife in Greece, Cleopatra fully realized that he had no other choice but to go. Yet she could not have been very happy about it. By now she had developed strong feelings for him, and there was no way to tell if he would ever return to Egypt. Moreover, she was pregnant once again, and the baby might never meet his or her father.

Despite these misgivings, after Antony's departure Cleopatra displayed no bitterness. True to her character, she remained both a realist and an optimist as well as eminently practical. For the moment, she knew that her best course was to concentrate on raising her children and ruling her kingdom, tasks she now tackled with considerable energy and effectiveness.

Chapter Four

EFFICIENT, SHREWD, AND RICH: CLEOPATRA AS A RULER

In the months and years following Caesar's assassination, and again in the months and years after Antony departed Alexandria, Cleopatra devoted most of her time and energy to administering her country. True, the queen was no doubt periodically distracted by what was going on in the corridors of Roman power. Her agents and spies kept her well apprised of what the Senate, Octavian, and especially her beloved Antony were up to. She learned, for instance, that in October 40 B.C., despite the earlier rebellion of Antony's wife and brother against Octavian, the two triumvirs had resolved their differences. Cleopatra likely took it in stride when these powerful men sealed the deal by signing a friendship pact (the Treaty of Brundisium, named after the Italian town where they concluded the agreement).

But the Egyptian queen must have been more than a little disturbed to hear that the deal made in Brundisium was also commemorated by Antony's marriage to Octa-

vian's sister, Octavia. (Fulvia had died in Greece shortly after Antony had joined her there, leaving him free to remarry.) In addition, it must have been especially difficult emotionally for Cleopatra when she gave birth to twins—Antony's children—only a few weeks after he married Octavia. (Cleopatra named the children Alexander Helios and Cleopatra Selene.)

Still, befitting her strong will and clarity of vision, Cleopatra managed to take these personal setbacks in her stride. In the spirit of a familiar old adage, what failed to destroy her appeared actually to make her stronger. She seemed to recognize that the well-being of her country, people, children, and throne now depended on her inner strength and ability to focus on affairs in the larger sphere beyond her personal needs and troubles. And the fact that she, a rare woman ruler in what was decidedly a man's world, could be so strong under the circumstances is a testament to her personal talents and toughness.

Not much is known about Cleopatra's specific domestic policies and acts during the years she ruled Egypt alone. This is partly because many ancient writers did not find the everyday workings of government noteworthy or interesting enough to record. Also, most administrative and economic documents of her reign have not survived. Some were purposely destroyed by the Romans after her death; others simply rotted away over the centuries.

The few shreds of reliable evidence that have survived suggest that Cleopatra was an efficient, practical, and at times even thoughtful ruler, who managed the economy well and treated her people justly. During her watch, in marked contrast to the reigns of her predecessors, there were no rebellions and tax collection proceeded normally. Moreover, she improved and expanded agriculture, producing large surpluses of grain and other foodstuffs, and she replenished the national treasury.

Antony Weds Octavia

In this passage from his biography of Antony (translated by Ian Scott-Kilvert in Makers of Rome*), Plutarch describes the circumstances under which Antony married Octavian's sister, Octavia.*

[O]ctavian] had a half-sister, Octavia, who was older than himself.... [He] was deeply attached to [her], who was, as the saying goes, a wonder of a woman. Her husband, Gaius Marcellus, had died only a short while before and she was now a widow, while Antony, since Fulvia's death, was also regarded as a widower. He did not deny his connection with Cleopatra, but ... in this matter he was still torn between his reason and his love for the Egyptian queen. Meanwhile, on the Roman side, everybody was anxious that this marriage [between Antony and Octavia] should take place, for it was hoped that ... this alliance would prove the salvation of their own [personal] affairs and would [also] restore harmony to the Roman world [by creating family connections between the two triumvirs].

This gold coin bearing Octavia's portrait was struck to celebrate the pact between Antony and Octavian.

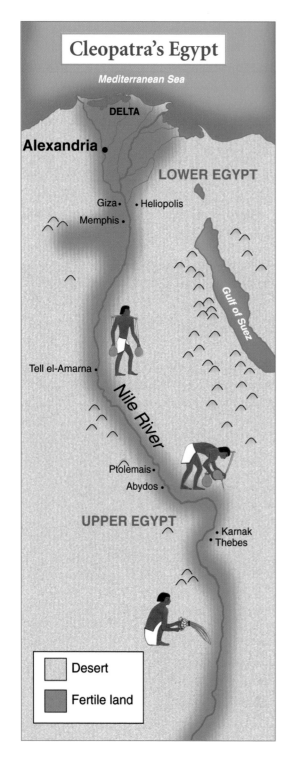

Cleopatra's Egypt

Mediterranean Sea

DELTA

Alexandria

LOWER EGYPT

Giza • • Heliopolis

Memphis •

Gulf of Suez

Tell el-Amarna •

Nile River

Ptolemais •

Abydos •

UPPER EGYPT

• Karnak
• Thebes

☐ Desert

■ Fertile land

Fair Tax Policies

It should be noted that Cleopatra's accomplishments in the domestic sphere were far from easy because nature worked against her at least part of the time. The first-century A.D. Roman writer, courtier, and philosopher Seneca the Younger recorded in his *Natural Questions*, "It is well established that in the reign of Cleopatra the Nile did not flood for two successive years, the tenth and eleventh of her reign [42 and 41 B.C.]."[35]

The failure of the Nile to flood was an extremely serious matter in Egypt. Each year, usually like clockwork, the river gently overflowed its banks and drenched farmers' fields with the freshwater needed to ensure healthy harvests. (Nearly all such fields were located in a narrow, fertile strip of land bordering the river's banks.) On the rare occasions when the river did not flood much or at all, catastrophic famine might be averted by distribution of extra grain stored in silos made of stone or baked clay. But some degree of famine in some regions of the country was inevitable. Moreover, a good deal of the money in Egypt's treasury came from overseas sales of grain. In such lean years, therefore, the government suffered a financial blow from which it had to find some way to recover.

It is noteworthy that Cleopatra did not try to make up for the economic shortages nature had caused by overtaxing her people, a tactic typical of other Ptolemaic rulers. The proof for this appears in a surviving decree, issued in her name (as well as in Caesarion's), on April 13, 41 B.C., at the height of floodwater crisis. "Nobody should demand of them [the farmers] anything above the essential Royal Dues [basic taxes]," the document begins,

> [or] attempt to act wrongfully and to include them among those of whom rural and provincial dues, which are not their concern, are exacted [collected]. We, being extremely indignant [about overtaxation] and considering it well to issue a General and Universal Ordinance [regulation] regarding the whole matter, have decreed that all those from the City [Alexandria], who carry on agricultural work in the country, shall not be subjected, as others are, to demands for *stephanoi* and *epigraphai* [gifts and special taxes people were traditionally forced to give the government] such as may be made from time to time. . . . Nor shall any new tax be required of them. But when they have once paid the essential dues, in kind [in the form of goods and services] or in cash, for cornland and for vineland . . . they shall not be molested for anything further, on any pretext whatever. Let it be done accordingly, and this [decree] put up in public, according to law.[36]

It must be emphasized that this decree seems specifically to address farmers who lived in and around Alexandria. The queen likely found it necessary to placate them first and foremost. After all, by virtue of their close proximity to the palace, people in the capital had more political voice and could cause more trouble by protesting than could people in the *chora*, or countryside. It is possible that Cleopatra issued one or more similar edicts for the rural food producers, but if so, none have yet been found.

Attempts at a Planned Economy

One might rightly ask how, if not through extra taxes, the queen expected to make up for the economic damage caused by one or two seasons of low crop yields. The answer may lie in her confidence that she could make the economic system her predecessors had put into place work better than they had. Here, it is important not to interpret the terms *economic system* and *economy* the way people do today. For the most part, the nation-states of the ancient world lacked large-scale, diversified economic systems featuring set financial theories and goals. In the words of noted historian M.I. Finley:

> Ancient society did not have an economic system which was an enormous conglomeration [assembly] of interdependent markets. . . . There were no business cycles. . . . Few [financial] records were normally retained once they had served their immediate purpose. Hence no time series [studies of economic trends over time] was available in antiquity, in either the public or the private sector . . . and without a time series there can be no reasoning by figures, no statistics.[37]

Without such statistics to study, the ancients could not plan financial strategy very far ahead or formulate theories about how to improve financial systems. So they tended, at least most of the time, to continue using the same agricultural, industrial, and commercial practices their ancestors had.

To their credit, several of the Ptolemaic rulers had attempted to go beyond this perpetuation of the economic status quo. Compared to the systems of other nations in the known world at the time, the Ptolemaic Egyptian version was perhaps the closest to a planned economy. The government at least tried to organize the farmers and other members of the country's labor force to ensure that production would be efficient and uninterrupted. Based on studies of various pieces of ancient literary and archaeological evidence, it appears that the government divided the land according to its productivity. The most productive land was leased to farmers who had to follow strict rules for how and when they sowed and harvested their grain. Government scribes kept careful track of the amounts of grain grown in various fields and decided how much of the harvest must be delivered to the state as a sort of rental fee for using the land. For less productive lands, the rules were less strict but were still enforced whenever possible.

In addition to these regulations for growing grain, Cleopatra's government maintained monopolies over the production of numerous other valuable commodities. These included oil (olive, sesame, linseed, safflower, and other varieties), textiles (wool, linen, and hemp), salt, and beer. The way the queen's agents ran these industries is well illustrated by the case of olive oil (used as fuel for lamps, as a cooking medium, as a skin cleaner, and as a base for various cosmetics). Once harvested, the olives went to state-regulated workrooms where the oil was extracted in presses. Then the queen's officials granted chosen individuals the right to sell the oil, under the condition that the government would receive a hefty portion of the profit. Evidence suggests that said profit ranged from 70 to 300 percent.

Mills that produced wool, along with wool sellers, worked under a similar arrangement. It is interesting to note that the chief official in charge of Cleopatra's wool mills was a Roman senator named Ovinius. This and other evidence indicate that, to increase efficiency and output, Cleopatra was willing to bring in foreign experts when appropriate rather than rely on less experienced native managers. It was partly through such increases in the efficiency of the existing system that the young queen was able to make up for the losses incurred by the Nile's failure to flood properly.

A Benevolent Dictator?

The Ptolemaic planned economy that Cleopatra administered so well had originally been designed, of course, to keep local Greeks in superior economic and social positions. Greeks traditionally received the best governmental positions, the most

A Land-Lease Contract

One of the more common business transactions that took place in Egypt under the Ptolemies, including Cleopatra, was the leasing of land by owners who collected rental income from those who lived on and actually worked it. This surviving contract from her reign (quoted in Jack Lindsay's study of Cleopatra) sealed such a deal between a Greek owner and a Persian tenant.

In the year 8 of Cleopatra['s reign] . . . Theon, son of Theon, of the katoikac cavalry, has leased to Apollonios . . . [a] Persian of Epigone, both being of the street of Cleopatra Aphrodite, the holding of 30 *arourai* [ancient units of land acreage] which belongs to him at Paimis, on condition that Apollonios shall sow [plant] half of it for year 9 with wheat and cultivate the other half with [another crop], at a rent for each aroura sown. . . . And Apollonios acknowledges that he has received from Theon the seed.

An Egyptian farmer plows his fields using a primitive plow pulled by oxen. His wife, tossing seeds, walks behind him.

productive farmlands, and so forth. Greeks also controlled most of the banking and loaned out most of the money the native peasants borrowed. Interest rates were very high—often 24 percent or more—which made paying back a loan a long and difficult affair. As a result, most natives could not escape their subsistence-level existence, but many Greeks enjoyed at least some degree of upward mobility.

By Cleopatra's time, however, the economic and social status of many Greeks in Egypt had diminished significantly. Over the centuries, the loss of parts of the old empire, increased economic competition from foreign lands, debasement of the currency, and other factors had taken a toll. They had forced large numbers of Greeks in Cleopatra's kingdom onto the same economic level as average native Egyptians. This may explain why Cleopatra was willing to reach out to native Egyptians (by learning their language and to some degree protecting them from tax collectors, for instance). In the yearly struggle for existence, they and most local Greeks were in the same boat, so to speak; and measures that helped one group helped the other.

It would be a mistake, however, to envision Cleopatra as a modern-style social and economic reformer fighting to aid the downtrodden. The fact is that she, like the vast majority of other ancient autocratic rulers, could not preserve her vast wealth and power without exploiting the labor and lives of large masses of common folk of minimal means. In general, it was necessary for such a ruler to maintain an extensive lower class (of peasants), a much smaller middle class (made up mostly of merchants and artisans), and a tiny, privileged upper class (of rulers and aristocrats).

Thus, as an absolute monarch Cleopatra's approach to rule seems to have been to create a sort of benevolent dictatorship. In such a scenario, the government relieves the burdens of the poor enough so that they see small but measurable improvement in their lives; that way they are likely to look on the ruler as a benefactor and be willing to work harder without complaint. But the ruler must not improve the lives of the commoners enough to allow true upward mobility and unlimited economic opportunity for all, as this would put more money in the people's hands at the expense of the royal treasury.

Dealings with Foreign Nations

However Cleopatra may have envisioned her role as a ruler, evidence shows that her attempts to institute or maintain sound economic policies in the domestic sphere were matched by some of her financial dealings with foreign states. In particular, some details of a transaction between her and Herod, king of Judaea (now Israel), have survived in the writings of the ancient Jewish historian Josephus. (At the time, Judaea was a Roman protectorate, a sort of puppet state in which Herod ran domestic affairs but followed Rome's bidding in foreign affairs.) Cleopatra and Herod did not like each other. But the Judaean ruler had to be

careful to treat her with respect because of her close relationship with Antony, the triumvir who controlled the East. Herod was well aware that Antony could, if given sufficient provocation, remove him from power, or even kill him, at any time.

The shrewd Cleopatra took full advantage of this situation. First, in a move that surely irritated Herod, Antony gave the queen a fertile tract of Judaean land that included the rich balsam-palm groves near the town of Jericho. During a trip to Judaea, Cleopatra met with Herod and it became clear that he was very anxious to regain use of these groves. According to Josephus, Herod tried giving the queen "costly gifts" and finally agreed to lease the land from her "at two hundred talents a year."[38] In this lopsided deal, Cleopatra retained ownership of the groves, and Herod had to pay her a huge yearly rental fee for using land that in his view belonged to him in the first place!

Herod had other reasons for disliking Cleopatra. His mother-in-law, Alexandra, hated him and wanted to replace him on the throne with her son, Aristoboulos. She asked Cleopatra to help advance this scheme by trying to convince Antony to oust Herod (in the mid–30s B.C., after Antony had returned to the East). Seeing Herod as a loyal and useful vassal, Antony refused to do so. But when Alexandra's plot failed and she was in danger, Cleopatra offered to give her asylum in Egypt, which further angered Herod.

A modern artist's conception of Herod, king of Judaea in Cleopatra's time.

Efficient, Shrewd, and Rich: Cleopatra as a Ruler 51

Showing Off Her Country's Riches

Meanwhile, Cleopatra continued to collect her rental fees from the disgruntled Judaean king and to expand Egyptian markets that exported grain, linen, and oil to various Mediterranean lands. Thanks to her sound economic policies, both domestic and foreign, the Egyptian treasury, which had been depleted under her predecessors, including her father, grew increasingly full. That made her government more solvent and better able to finance large-scale projects. Of these, the biggest launched outside Egypt's borders was Antony's Parthian campaign, to which she contributed enormous amounts of money and supplies.

Inside her country, in contrast, Cleopatra oversaw several major building projects

Cleopatra Acquires Land in Judaea

In this excerpt from his Jewish War *(G.A. Williamson's translation), the ancient Jewish historian Josephus, who disliked Cleopatra as much as his Greek and Roman counterparts, gave his version of her acquisition of the palm groves near Jericho.*

[Antony] sliced off large parts of [the territories of various eastern rulers], including the palm-groves at Jericho in which the balsam is produced, and gave them to Cleopatra along with all the cities [in the region], except Tyre and Sidon. . . . Mistress now of this domain, she escorted Antony as far as the Euphrates [River] on his way to fight the Parthians, and then came [back] via Apamea and Damascus into Judaea. Herod placated her hostility with costly gifts, and leased back from her the lands broken off from his kingdom, at two hundred talents a year!

Jewish historian Josephus Flavius criticized Antony's generosity toward the Egyptian pharaoh, Cleopatra.

Early modern Egyptians in the ruins of ancient Alexandria. The obelisk, often called "Cleopatra's Needle," was transported to New York in 1879.

of various kinds. Perhaps the most famous and splendid was the construction of the Caesareum—a special temple in the heart of Alexandria to honor the memory of her first lover-ally, Caesar. When this impressive structure was completed (by Cleopatra's enemy, Octavian, following her untimely death in 30 B.C.), its entrance was marked by two towering obelisks, which have come to be called "Cleopatra's Needles."[39] Originally carved by the pharaoh Thutmosis III more than fourteen centuries before, each stood sixty-nine feet high and weighed almost two hundred tons. The ancient Alexandrian writer Philo describes the rest of the temple this way:

There is elsewhere no sanctuary like that which is called the Caesareum, a temple to Caesar . . . situated on a spit of land facing the [city's] harbors famed for their excellent moorings, huge and conspicuous, forming an area of vast breadth, embellished with porticoes [roofed walkways], libraries, men's banqueting halls, groves . . . spacious courts, open-air rooms, in short everything which lavish expenditure could produce to beautify it—the whole a hope of safety to the voyager whether going into or out of the harbor.[40]

Another way that Cleopatra showed off the country's replenished riches, as well as her personal power and prestige, was by giving lavish state dinners like those she and Antony had enjoyed. The second-century Greek historian Socrates of Rhodes provides this description of the incredible splendor of one such banquet:

The service was wholly of gold and jeweled vessels made with exquisite art; even the walls were hung with tapestries woven of gold and silver threads.... Each [of the guests] was allowed to take away the couch on which he had lain [while eating].

Even the sideboards, as well as the couch-spreads, were divided among the guests.... [For a single banquet] she distributed fees amounting to a talent [the equivalent of nearly twenty years' pay to the average worker in those days] for the purchase of roses; the floors of the dining rooms were strewn with them a cubit [roughly twenty inches] deep, in net-like festoons spread over everything.[41]

Cleopatra's magnificent lifestyle, along with her effective policies as a ruler, illuminated the tremendous transformation she had undergone in a mere decade. An exiled young princess desperate to regain her lost throne had grown into a major player on the international political stage and the richest, most powerful woman in the world.

Chapter Five

MASTER PROPAGANDIST: CLEOPATRA MOLDS HER OWN IMAGE

Seen both by the Egyptian people during Cleopatra's reign and by unbiased observers looking back from later times and places, one of the most striking aspects of her rule was the public image she projected. The official portrait had three key dimensions. First, the queen was a compassionate mother figure who cared about and carefully maintained the welfare of her people. Second, despite being a woman (a gender viewed as inherently weak by nearly everyone before the modern era), she was strong enough both to defend the nation and to expand its borders and influence. Last, and certainly not least, was a point that reinforced the first two: Namely, she possessed a direct connection with the divine forces watching over human affairs. In other words, as a chosen representative of the gods, she knew what was best for Egypt and indeed for the greater world beyond its borders.

It is taken for granted today that movie stars, politicians, and other people in the public spotlight hire public relations experts who carefully craft and tweak their public images. There is nothing new or unusual about this. Kings, queens, generals, presidents, and other leaders have done it throughout recorded history, and it would be surprising if Cleopatra had not done so. What made her stand out from many historical figures in this regard was her unusual personal talent for public relations. Although she no doubt had advisers who coached her in this department, evidence suggests that she directed the molding of her public image (as well as those of Caesarion and her other children) mainly on her own. Moreover, in an age and place

Cleopatra frequently depicted herself in the company of powerful goddesses, including Hathor, seen in this relief from the Temple of Dendera.

in which most people could not read, she did this primarily through the expert manipulation of visual images. As Lucy Hughes-Hallett points out:

> Cleopatra was as adroit as Octavian [who later proved himself a master propagandist] in shaping the public perception of her own actions. Like him, she deliberately imposed on them an imaginary meaning designed to enhance her perceived image, to justify her policies, and to further her cause. Unlike him, she did not use words, which were inaccessible to the illiterate majority [of her people.

Instead, she used] the language of drama and spectacle. Between the lines of the ancient accounts of her career one can watch a fantastic pageant being performed, a pageant which is simultaneously a sequence of real events and the symbolic and immensely exaggerated representation of them. . . . Cleopatra's spectacles were . . . designed to impress spectators with the power and glory of their originator.[42]

Beneath the Hype

In fact, the famous queen did such a good job of shaping public perceptions about her that modern observers are at a disadvantage. In the process, she enhanced the veil of mystery and romanticism that has

The Berlin Bust of Cleopatra

The portrait is in fine condition, except for one or two small abrasions. . . . [It] follows the type [of image of the queen] found on the coins of Alexandria . . . [and] is a slightly more flattering portrayal of the queen than the Vatican [bust]. . . . Cleopatra is shown with the usual melon hairstyle [in which the hair is gathered in a bun] and a broad diadem [jeweled band]. Unlike the Vatican portrait, however, her diadem is set further back on the head, and runs underneath her bun. . . . The Berlin head's nose has a slightly downturned tip with curving

The Berlin bust of Cleopatra shows a woman with strong, attractive features and a look of confidence and determination.

nostrils that compare favorably with the portraits of Cleopatra VII on coins and clay sealings. The mouth is downturned at the corners, the lower lip somewhat fleshier than the upper.

surrounded her ever since. And trying to find surviving evidence that shows what she was like as a private or "real" person is extremely difficult. The problem has been greatly compounded, of course, by the negative counterimage created by the Romans during and after her lifetime. In their very effective propaganda, they portrayed Cleopatra as scheming, murderous, power hungry, and dishonest. And the combination of the positive image she crafted of herself and the negative one the Romans projected in large degree obscures the real person beneath all the hype.

Before examining how Cleopatra carefully crafted her public image, it is useful first to try to paint a brief picture of the person behind the facade. Scattered among the tracts of negative Roman propaganda about her are clues to her real character. First, there is Plutarch's observation that she became fluent in the Egyptian language. He and other ancient writers also suggested that she could read and write as many as eight languages in all. If true, she must have been remarkably intelligent and articulate. Indeed, Plutarch's remark that she was a delight to converse with seems to confirm this.

Cleopatra's actions as a ruler are also revealing clues that undercut the hype to some degree. In Hughes-Hallett's words, "Her character can best be deduced from the way she conducted her career."[43] First, her raising of an army to regain her throne after her exile in the early 40s B.C. shows that she was resourceful, feisty, and brave. She was also a steadfast and trustworthy friend. This is proven by her unwavering loyalty to Caesar, and later to Antony, no matter how difficult the circumstances became. She was also faithful as a lover. Despite the fact that Cleopatra was often portrayed by the Romans as a temptress, evidence proves that she only had intimate relationships with Caesar and Antony. Moreover, she bore children by both men and seems to have been a caring, attentive mother.

At the same time, there seems little doubt that Cleopatra was an ambitious person who was willing to resort to forceful, even ruthless means to further her political aims. Historically such traits and behavior have been readily accepted, even admired, in male leaders but deplored and denounced in female ones. A person must judge for him- or herself, therefore, whether Cleopatra's sometimes aggressive political policies and tactics were negative or positive traits. Her ultimate goal may have been personal glory and gratification, as Roman writers would have us believe. But it could just as well have been the glorification and preservation of her people and country. After all, she lived in a hostile world in which Greek-ruled kingdoms were an endangered species. (Rome had recently defeated or intimidated into submission nearly all of the other Greek states.)

What Did Cleopatra Look Like?

There seems little doubt, therefore, that, whatever the motives that drove her, the real Cleopatra was a smart, shrewd, strong-willed woman. She was capable of forming loving, lasting relationships and was willing and able to do whatever was necessary to promote the well-being of her family and country. How did she incorporate these and her other real personal traits into the public image she projected?

First, the queen's public relations strategy was, by necessity, shaped to some degree by her physical attributes. If she had been abnormally short, for example, she might have adopted the habits of wearing high-heeled footwear or always remaining seated when in the public eye; or, if she had been extremely homely, she might have hidden behind veils while in public and developed an official cover story to explain her use of such coverings.

No evidence suggests that Cleopatra was short, ugly, or had any other unusual physical drawbacks. But what *did* she look like? Although Plutarch briefly described her charming, magnetic personality, he did not provide a clear physical description of her, nor did any other ancient writer. To get some idea of what she looked like, therefore, we must turn to artistic and archaeological evidence. These take the form of portrait busts and facial images on coins, all of which were used to define the images of and mold public opinion about ancient rulers.

A number of ancient busts purporting to depict Cleopatra can be found in various museums around the world. However, none have yet been proven authentic to the satisfaction of the vast majority of scholars. Of the two most likely candidates,

One of a number of unauthenticated ancient portrait busts of Cleopatra.

the leading one presently resides in the Vatican Museum in Rome. Found in 1784 in the ruins of a Roman villa in Italy, it shows a young woman with her hair pulled back in a bun. The nose is missing. But the chin, lips, and forehead are those of a well-proportioned, moderately attractive face. The other bust, which rests in a museum in Berlin, Germany, strongly resembles the Vatican bust. The major exception is that the nose is intact on the Berlin bust. These sculptures, noted British Museum scholar Susan Walker writes,

> have lost their torsos and offer no sense of Cleopatra's dress and jewelry. . . . [If they are indeed authentic, they] suggest Cleopatra's youth, and could date from the early years of her reign. . . . Both works . . . [might have been created during] Cleopatra's extended stay in Rome as Caesar's guest from 46 to 44 B.C.[44]

A majority of scholars think that the images on a handful of surviving coins are more authentic likenesses of the famous Egyptian queen's face. Most of these coins are too worn to make out any details, but about ten are in reasonably good condition. The faces depicted on them are remarkably similar. All have a prominent chin, a long, slightly hooked nose, and wavy hair tied back in a bun. This suggests that they all depict the same person and that this image was at least an officially approved portrait of the queen, if not necessarily a 100 percent accurate one. Ernle Bradford gives this excellent description of one of the best examples, a copper coin minted in Alexandria:

> [The coin] shows Cleopatra when young, depicts her wearing the diadem [crown] of monarchy, and with her hair arranged in a bun at the nape of her neck. The neck itself is long, strong, and graceful. The general appearance of her features is of neatness and deli-

cacy, with fine large eyes. The famous nose is not as long as it appears in some other coin portraits, but is definitely more Semitic than classical Greek. . . . The overall impression one gets from this and other coins at later stages of her life, is of a good-looking, but not pretty, woman. The eyes, the height of the brow, the clarity of the features, the nose and chin, all suggest a woman of intellect and power—which indeed she was. . . . This is the face of dignity—the face of a queen.[45]

An Extremely Religious People

Part of Cleopatra's public image was therefore shaped by her likenesses on coins and statues. This gave her subjects a rough idea of what she looked like. But by itself this was not enough to create feelings of awe, respect, and allegiance among the people. To inspire such strong emotions, she needed to project a larger-than-life image and, if possible, one that transcended, or went beyond, life. By her time, the vast majority of Egyptians did not think that the pharaohs who ruled them were divine beings (a belief that had died out more than a thousand years before). However, many ancient rulers, including the Ptolemaic kings and queens who had preceded Cleopatra on the Egyptian throne, went to great lengths to establish that they had some special connection to the gods.

One way they did this was by sponsoring the Ptolemaia, a religious festival accompanied by athletic games, every four

Death for Killing a Cat

One reason that Cleopatra was able to exploit religion so well in her propaganda was that the Egyptian people were extremely devout. One of the most famous incidents illustrating their deep respect for the gods and religious traditions was reported by the Greek historian Diodorus Siculus, who visited Egypt in the late first century B.C. when Cleopatra was a young woman. He was an eyewitness when an angry crowd of locals chased and captured a Roman visitor who had accidentally killed a cat. Cats were sacred to the Egyptians and the killing of one was seen as an unpardonable sin. Thus, even though the king's agents came and pleaded with them to spare the man's life (for fear that Rome might retaliate against Egypt), these religious vigilantes lynched their captive.

The Egyptians were devoutly religious, as illustrated by paintings of gods like this one.

years. It was inspired by and similar in many ways to the Olympic Games held in southern Greece every four years. The events in both included running, jumping, wrestling, chariot racing, and so on. The main difference was that, whereas the Olympics honored Zeus, leader of the Greek gods, the Egyptian version honored the major Egyptian gods, along with the Ptolemaic rulers themselves. In the grand procession that opened the festival, priests and their attendants carried magnificent images of the gods. Mixed in with these (and often even preceding them) were paintings and sculpted portraits of the Ptolemies, past and present. The intent was not to suggest that these human rulers *were* gods, but that the gods approved of and supported them and their policies. It was potent propaganda, and Cleopatra took full advantage of it.

The main reason such spectacles were so effective was that the Egyptian people were extremely religious. According to the fifth-century B.C. Greek historian Herodotus, who visited Egypt, "They are religious to excess, beyond any other nation in the world."[46] For this reason, Cleopatra not only celebrated the four-yearly Ptolemaia, but she also went to great lengths to maintain good relations with the nation's priests and to observe traditional Egyptian religious rites.

The New Isis

In fact, the shrewd and gutsy queen also went a daring step further by actually equating herself with the country's most popular goddess—Isis. A fertility goddess, Isis was thought to oversee the growth and harvesting of wheat and barley (crops essential to Egypt's well-being). She was also seen as a caring, benevolent mother figure, frequently portrayed in art nurturing her young son, Horus (an image that strongly influenced early Christian images of Mary holding the baby Jesus). In addition, Isis was associated with forgiveness of sins and other kinds of religious purification and salvation. In his popular novel, *The Golden Ass*, the Roman writer Apuleius describes the way the goddess's adherents pictured her:

> To begin with, she had a full head of hair which hung down, gradually curling as it spreads loosely and flows gently over her divine neck. Her lofty head was encircled by a garland interwoven with diverse blossoms, at the center of which above her brow was a flat disk resembling a mirror, or rather the orb of the moon, which emitted a glittering light. The crown was held in place by coils of rearing snakes . . . and adorned above with waving ears of corn. She wore a multicolored dress woven from fine linen, one part of which shone radiantly white, a second glowed yellow with saffron blossom, and a third blazed rosy red. . . . [A] jet-black cloak gleamed with a dark sheen as it enveloped her. . . . The garment hung down in layers of successive folds, its lower edge gracefully undulating [rippling] with tasseled fringes. . . . Her feet, divinely white, were shod in sandals fashioned from the leaves of the palm of victory. Such, then, was the appearance of the mighty goddess.[47]

At some time during her reign, Cleopatra began to take on this traditionally accepted appearance of Isis whenever she was in public. On such occasions, Plutarch writes, she "wore the [black] robe which is sacred to Isis, and she was addressed [by her subjects] as the New Isis."[48] She even went so far as to issue a set of coins showing her in the guise of the popular goddess. It is important to understand how Cleopatra identified herself with and simultaneously distinguished herself from Isis. Most people in the ancient world accepted that a particular deity could have several different manifestations—in essence, separate parts of the same personality. The queen therefore presented herself as an earthly manifestation of Isis, in a way a semidivine agent of the goddess sent to improve humanity's lot.

The use of the word *humanity* here is crucial. By Cleopatra's day the worship of Isis had spread across the Mediterranean world and encompassed hundreds of thousands of Greeks, Romans, and others. Her father, Auletes, had not grasped the potential of exploiting this phenomenon to his advan-

This set of gold and lapis lazuli figures portrays the divine family of Osiris, Isis, and Horus, gods with whom Cleopatra tried to associate her own family.

tage. However, Cleopatra, a master propagandist, did see this potential. Her close relationships with powerful Romans had made her famous throughout the known world. And she no doubt hoped that her identification with Isis would make her more acceptable in Italy and other places where the natives were suspicious of foreigners.

New Myths for a Future King

Cleopatra also worked hard to create a powerful and positive public image for her son Caesarion. If she was the new Isis, it followed that her son by Caesar was the new Horus. The propagation of this parallel was aided by the association of the dead Caesar with Osiris,

divine husband of Isis and father of Horus. (In Egyptian myths, Osiris, like Caesar, had been brutally murdered in his prime.)

Cleopatra created her updated, parallel mythology partly by issuing a coin showing her as Isis suckling the baby Caesarion-Horus. More potent were carved images of Cleopatra and Caesarion mingled with those of gods in selected temples. Perhaps the most influential was the display in the Temple of Hathor at Dendera (a few miles north of the ancient capital of Thebes), described by Michael Foss:

> Here, in colossal relief, stand Queen Cleopatra and in front of her a full-scale male named as Ptolemy Caesar. They bear gifts of musical instruments and gold which they are offering to Hathor . . . goddess of music and love. . . . The noble figure standing in front of Ptolemy Caesar is Isis . . . the consort and savior of Osiris, who brings the slaughtered god back to life and is then delivered of his divine child. . . . The holy message, therefore . . . was [that] Isis-Cleopatra had conceived out of the dead god Osiris-Caesar . . . and the child of their union was Horus-Caesarion, now properly called Ptolemy Caesar, and divinely appointed co-ruler of the Two lands of Egypt. And this was the king destined in the future . . . to reconcile under one crown the two empires of Egypt and Rome.[49]

Opposite: Cleopatra's own effective propaganda partially endures in modern images like this one, which idealize her.

Writing and Performing in Her Own Legend

In examining such examples of Cleopatra's adept use of public relations to enhance her and her family's images, it is noteworthy that a number of books were attributed to her in ancient and medieval times. They covered a wide range of subjects, including philosophy, medicine, weights and measures, science, and cosmetics. The latter work contained a popular cure for baldness that some Europeans employed well into late medieval times. Many of these books were probably assigned to Cleopatra centuries after her death as part of the growing mystique that surrounded her. But some of them may have been part of her own propaganda. It is possible that she had someone write the book on cosmetics, for example, and then put her name on it to advertise both her literacy and literary talents. (None of these works have survived in their entirety, and none can be positively linked to Cleopatra.)

Cleopatra's masterful use of propaganda, like that of her Roman enemies later, demonstrates that "the art of public relations is a very ancient one," Hughes-Hallett writes. This partly explains why Cleopatra became such a larger-than-life figure both in her own and later times. She and her opponents "treated the events in which they participated as the raw material of propaganda and myth," and "moment by moment they were writing, directing, and performing in their own legends, even in the act of living out their lives."[50]

Chapter Six

CHALLENGER OF ROME: CLEOPATRA VERSUS OCTAVIAN

Aside from her reputation as a mysterious seducer of men, Cleopatra is most famous for her military stand, along with Antony, against the Roman colossus. This bold bid for power had only two possible outcomes. Either the lovers would win and assume control of most of the known world; or they would lose and be utterly destroyed. The fact that she threw herself and all of her resources into such an enormous gamble speaks volumes about her courage, determination, and sheer audaciousness.

But how did Antony, who had left Cleopatra and married Octavian's sister, end up siding with the Egyptian queen against his own country? In 37 B.C. Antony left Octavia in Rome and traveled to Syria to prepare for his long-anticipated invasion of Parthia. No sooner had he landed, when he sent for Cleopatra. He did so partly because they still had a deal that she would aid him in his upcoming campaign. But it cannot be discounted that he also

remembered their good times together. In fact, Plutarch may have been right in saying that Antony still loved, or at least felt passion for, Cleopatra. This passion, Plutarch writes, "had lain dormant in his heart," and now "suddenly gathered strength and blazed once more into life."[51]

Whatever Antony's motivations at the time, once he was reunited with Cleopatra, the two remained close allies and lovers ever after. She stuck with him even after his military venture in Parthia, launched in 36 B.C., ended in abject failure. (It appears that he planned to try again at some later opportune time.) Not surprisingly, the lover's steadfast alliance placed them on a direct collision course with Octavian, who took advantage of the situation by claiming that Antony had abandoned Rome for the Egyptian queen. Both sides ultimately had the same goal—mastery of the Mediterranean world. And both were willing to fight another civil war to achieve that goal. Moreover, both were more or less evenly matched, not only in military might but also in their mastery of propaganda designed to demonize and demoralize each other.

Antony Bewitched?

Octavian certainly had plenty of grist for his own propaganda mill. Antony's abandonment of Octavia, who had a reputation for virtue and kindness and was well loved by the Roman public, was a black mark against his own reputation. He did not love Octavia and had married her only to help facilitate the treaty he had signed with Octavian. So the hurt feelings and public embarrassment Antony caused her were of little consequence to him. In fact, once he was reunited with Cleopatra and had established a new headquarters in Athens, Greece, he made it clear to Octavia that he would not return to her. (At Cleopatra's urgings, he eventually divorced her and even went so far as to have his agents physically evict her from their home in Rome.)

Needless to say, this callous behavior, which most Romans viewed as cold and cruel, played right into Octavian's hands. The shrewd young heir to Caesar's name and political following had been looking for some wedge to drive between Antony and the Roman people. And Antony seemed to be handing him that wedge on a proverbial platter. Following Antony's rejection of Octavia, Octavian wasted no time in launching a large-scale and highly effective propaganda campaign against his rival.

In one of the opening salvos of this public relations attack, Octavian claimed he had come into possession of a copy of Antony's will. Whether the document was genuine or, as is more likely, a clever forgery engineered by Octavian's henchmen, will never be known. What is certain is that the Roman Senate accepted its authenticity, as did the majority of average Romans.

This idealized statue of Octavian was created after Cleopatra's death, when he had become Augustus.

The supposed will stated that Antony wanted to be buried in Cleopatra's tomb in Alexandria instead of in his native Italy. Moreover, the will said that Caesarion, now about eleven years old, was Caesar's legitimate son, which meant that he, an Egyptian prince, and not Octavian, a full-blooded Roman, was the rightful heir to Caesar's titles, lands, and powers.

Octavian not only damaged Antony's reputation by releasing the contents of this probably trumped up will, but he also denounced Cleopatra and her supposed corruption of a once noble Roman leader. The wicked queen had bewitched Antony, Octavian claimed. Further, she and her nefarious aides had drugged him so that he was little more than putty in their treacherous anti-Roman hands. "Antony was no longer responsible for his actions," as Plutarch puts it, and Cleopatra and her low-life cronies "were mainly responsible for the direction of affairs [in the East]." [52]

Antony and Cleopatra were surely not pleased with the way Octavian was distorting their characters. But apparently they were confident that they could defeat him in the end. The lovers continued to cement their ties with each other, both politically and personally, which provided Octavian with still more valuable fuel for his propaganda machine. On the one hand, Antony gave Cleopatra control over several eastern territories without the consent of the Roman government. On the other, in January 35 B.C. Cleopatra gave birth to her third child by Antony, a boy they named Ptolemy Philadelphus. In addition, Octavian's spies reported that Antony had begun wearing Egyptian clothes and had become little more than the queen's servant. Dio Cassius later wrote that Cleopatra had

> enslaved him so completely that . . . she was saluted by him as . . . "mistress" and she had Roman soldiers [Antony's men] in her bodyguard, all of whom had her name inscribed upon their shield. . . . These and other outrageous practices] gave the impression that she had laid him under some spell and deprived him of his wits. [53]

Kings and Queens of the East

Meanwhile, Cleopatra and Antony were creating propaganda of their own on an equally large scale. Theirs consisted less of denunciations of Octavian and more of measures designed to make themselves appear to be invincible, heaven-sent beings who were destined to rule not only the East but the whole world. The intent seems to have been to consolidate the tremendous human and material resources of the East behind them. That would allow them eventually to turn that vast region into their personal empire, one that would overshadow the western Roman sphere.

Part and parcel in this effort was Cleopatra's ongoing equation of herself with Isis and Caesarion with Horus. At the same time, Antony, who had long identified himself in the East with the Greek fertility god Dionysus (the Roman Bacchus) played up his connection with this mysterious and popular deity. He issued coins showing himself dressed as Dionysus, which complemented those Cleopatra had issued showing herself in Isis's guise. The couple also raised statues of themselves as Dionysus and Isis, including an imposing pair atop the famous Acropolis in Athens.

The climax of this immense propaganda campaign occurred in 34 B.C. Cleopatra and Antony staged a spectacular and lavish public ceremony that became known as the Donations of Alexandria, which was attended by enormous crowds of Egyptians as well as visitors from neighboring lands. Plutarch tells how, at the height of the show, Antony granted several more eastern lands to his and Cleopatra's children, an act bound to infuriate Octavian and his supporters back in Rome:

He assembled a great multitude in the athletic arena and had two thrones of gold, one for himself and one for Cleopatra, placed on a dais [platform] of silver, with smaller thrones for his children. First, he proclaimed Cleopatra queen of Egypt, Cyprus, Lybia, and Coele-Syria, and named Caesarion as her consort. . . . Next he proclaimed his own sons by Cleopatra to be Kings of Kings. To Alexander [Helios] he gave Armenia, Media, and Parthia, as soon as he should have conquered it,

This nineteenth-century English painting depicts Antony approaching Cleopatra's pleasure barge. He ended up betraying Rome for her.

and to Ptolemy [Philadephus], Phoenicia, Syria, and Cilicia. At the same time he presented his sons to the people, Alexander in a Median costume …and Ptolemy …wore Macedonian dress like the kings who succeeded Alexander the Great. . . . [Cleopatra] wore the robe which is sacred to Isis.[54]

Predictably, typical reactions back in Italy to this display were shock, indignation, and anger, thanks in large degree to Octavian's adept manipulation of news and public opinion. Plutarch writes that Octavian "did his utmost to rouse the Roman people's anger against"[55] Antony. And Dio says that most Romans were so outraged that "they were willing to believe other rumors current at the time," among these that Antony "would hand over the city of Rome to Cleopatra and transfer the seat of government to Egypt."[56]

A New Golden Age?

Cleopatra and Antony were quick to counter this barrage of propaganda with more of their own, this time through the clever manipulation of an ancient prophecy. For centuries, priests and writers in various Mediterranean lands had predicted the coming of a golden age, a new world order in which wars and crime would be eliminated and happy times would prevail. Integral to these tales was the emergence of a special leader, usually associated in some way with the sun. Until his unexpected death, millions of people had been convinced that Alexander the Great was this

new leader. (Later many would see Jesus Christ as the fulfillment of the prophecy.)

Resurrecting the prophecy, Cleopatra and Antony augmented it by drawing attention to a poem written in 40 B.C. by the great Roman writer Virgil. This work, the *Fourth Eclogue*, predicted the birth of a special, divine boy who would usher in a new age of peace and "free the Earth from never-ceasing fear. He shall receive the life of the gods, and . . . and himself be seen [among] them."[57] Virgil had written these words to commemorate the Treaty of Brundisium. His intent was to suggest that the marriage of Antony and Octavia would produce a child with the "superior" blood of two powerful triumvirs. It was hoped that that child would grow up to rule a new and better Roman world.

This original context of the poem became lost in Cleopatra's and Antony's propaganda blitz. In their version, Cleopatra, not Octavia, was the mother of the coming boy-savior. That semidivine child now became young Alexander Helios, who shared the names of both the great conqueror and the Greek sun god (Helios). For many people in the East, this seemed to reinforce the notion that Cleopatra and Antony were destined to lay the foundation for a wondrous new age in which Rome and the East would merge into one vast, peaceful land.

On the Eve of War

By 32 B.C., therefore, the Mediterranean sphere was divided, polarized into two vast opposing camps, one commanded by

Octavian, the other by Cleopatra and Antony. (By this time, Octavian and Antony had deposed the third triumvir, Lepidus, who remained under house arrest for the rest of his days.) Each side was inflexible in its position, so a war that would decide the ultimate fate of the known world seemed inevitable. In retrospect, knowing that Octavian won, it is easy to forget that at the time the outcome of the conflict was far from certain. Octavian had many troops and ample resources on which to draw. But he was well aware that his opponents were potentially even stronger. Cleopatra and Antony had thousands of Roman troops then stationed in the East, along with large numbers of soldiers and ships from numerous eastern provinces and kingdoms. Added to this were the immense stores of grain and money of Egypt. Still another factor working in favor of the lovers was the fact that Antony retained the support of a considerable number of Roman leaders who did not like or trust Octavian. In the spring of 32 B.C., the two consuls (Rome's jointly serving administrator-generals) and nearly three hundred senators (accompanied by thousands of followers) left Rome and joined Antony.

What worked against Cleopatra and Antony in the long run was overconfidence in their vast resources, coupled with Octavian's bold seizure of the initiative. First, Antony was too slow in assembling his forces. He and the Egyptian queen decided to spend some time in Greece, where

they held more large-scale ceremonies intended to promote their power and prestige. In Plutarch's words, this casual approach on the eve of war "is now considered to have been one of [Antony's] greatest errors of judgment, since it gave Octavian the opportunity to complete his [military] preparations."[58]

Another factor in Octavian's favor was a sort of human secret weapon—his leading military commander, Marcus Vipsanius Agrippa. Though a fairly young man

A late medieval Italian bust of the great Roman poet Virgil.

more than 100,000 land troops. However, Agrippa also realized that Antony's ships were mostly larger, heavier, and thus slower and less maneuverable. Also, Agrippa planned to employ some novel offensive weapons of his own design. These included big catapults that hurled flaming material to set afire the sails and decks of enemy ships.

Ready for the fight, Octavian and Agrippa hastily advanced their forces on Greece at a time when their opponents' army and navy were still disorganized and unprepared. In March 31 B.C. Agrippa attacked and captured the port of Methone, located on Greece's southern coast, one of Antony's main naval bases. Agrippa also directed his fleet to disrupt Antony's supply lines to the east. Simultaneously, Octavian led his land forces into Greece and established a large camp near Actium, on the peninsula's western coast.

A sixteenth-century painting depicts Cleopatra and Antony feasting.

Cleopatra's Military Advice

Cleopatra and Antony had not anticipated these swift and bold initiatives by the enemy and now found themselves bottled up in Greece. Clearly, there was little choice but to fight their way out of the trap. But which strategy would be best to achieve this goal—a land battle or a sea battle?

Antony's second in command, Canidius Crassus, argued that the most logical and effective option was to abandon the fleet and confront Octavian on land. Plutarch

(then only about thirty), Agrippa was shrewd, inventive, and had already amassed a great deal of battle experience. At his disposal were about 250 lightweight, very maneuverable warships and some 80,000 land troops. He knew that Antony's forces were larger—more than 500 ships and

reports that Crassus advised Antony to send Cleopatra away to some safe haven and then meet the enemy somewhere in northern Greece.

There would be no disgrace, Canidius urged, in giving up the control of the sea to Octavian, since his forces had been trained in naval operations during [some battles Agrippa had recently fought against rebels in the West]. On the other hand, it would be absurd for Antony, who was as experienced in fighting on land as any commander living, not to take advantage of the superior numbers and equipment of his army, but to distribute his fighting men among the ships and so fritter away his strength.[59]

The confidence that Antony had in Cleopatra and her judgment, even in military matters, is proven by the fact that he took her advice over Crassus's. She insisted that they must fight at sea. Octavian and Agrippa would like nothing better than to draw their opponents away from their ships and into the Greek countryside, she likely argued. There, Antony's troops would be ill supplied and forced to live off the land, and the enemy would refuse to engage them as long as possible in an attempt to wear them down. Disaster would ultimately ensue. By contrast, a naval encounter would at least afford them an even chance of breaking out of the trap. In retrospect, this seems like sound advice, and it is not surprising that Antony acted on it.

The Showdown at Actium

The ensuing battle took place on September 2, 31 B.C., off the Greek coast near Actium. At first, because of a lack of wind, the opposing fleets kept their distance from each other and remained idle. During this tense lull, the commanders on both sides attempted to beef up their troops' morale. "Antony made the round of all the ships in a small rowing boat," Plutarch writes. "He urged the soldiers to rely on the weight of their vessels [which were mostly larger than those of the enemy] and to stand firm and fight exactly as if they were on land."[60] Meanwhile, in addressing his own troops, Octavian (according to Dio) berated Antony, saying:

He is either blind to reason or mad, for I have heard and can believe that he is bewitched by that accursed woman.... And so, being enslaved by her, he plunges into war . . . for her sake, against ourselves and against his country. What choice, then, remains to us, save our duty to oppose him, together with Cleopatra?[61]

By early afternoon, there was no more time for speeches, as the wind finally picked up and Antony ordered his ships to attack. According to Dio, who based his account on the testimony of eyewitnesses:

At the sound of the trumpet Antony's fleet began to move, and, keeping close together, formed their line. . . . [Soon afterwards, Octavian] made a signal and, advancing both his wings [groups

of- ships on the far left and right], rounded his line in the form of an enveloping crescent. [Dio makes it sound as if Octavian personally conceived this strategy; in reality, Agrippa formulated the plan and directed their ships.] His object was to encircle the enemy if possible or, if not, at least to break up their formation. Antony was alarmed by this outflanking and encircling maneuver, moved forward to meet it as best he could, and so unwillingly joined battle with Octavian.[62]

As the fleets bore down on each other, Antony managed to lengthen his front line of ships by at least half a mile, which foiled the enemy's attempt to encircle his fleet. Minutes later, the two fleets met head on. Few of the vessels tried to ram one another, which was unusual since the chief offensive naval tactic of ancient times was to build up a burst of speed and ram the opposing vessel. In this case, however, most of Antony's ships were too big and heavy to build up the necessary speed; and some of Octavian's vessels avoided ramming runs when they saw that the hulls of the enemy ships were protected by metal plates. In many cases, therefore, the opposing forces concentrated on getting close enough to kill people on enemy decks or to grab hold of a vessel and board

it. "Octavian's ships resembled cavalry," Dio writes,

now launching a charge, and now retreating, since they could attack or draw off [opposing vessels] as they chose, while Antony's were like heavy infantry, warding off the enemy's efforts to ram them, but also striving to hold them with their grappling-hooks.[63]

Plutarch agreed that the fight in many ways resembled "a land battle." Three or more "of Octavian's ships clustered round each of Antony's, and the fighting was carried on with . . . spears, poles, and flaming missiles."[64]

An Awful Truth

As Antony's ships engaged the enemy vessels in the front lines, Cleopatra's squadron of sixty ships waited in reserve a few thousand feet farther back. It appears that the plan was for her contingent to do one of two things, depending on how the struggle went. If Antony's ships defeated the enemy's, her vessels would move in to rescue any of Antony's sailors who were in the water. If, on the other hand, the battle seemed lost, Cleopatra's squadron would try to break out and escape. The queen also had the task of guarding a vast cache of gold and jewels on her flagship, a treasure essential to her and Antony's further prosecution of the war.

As it turned out, Cleopatra chose the second option—escape. And Antony followed

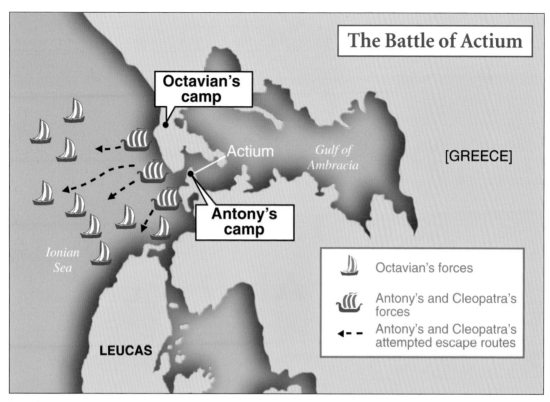

The Battle of Actium

Octavian's camp

Actium

Gulf of Ambracia

[GREECE]

Antony's camp

Ionian Sea

LEUCAS

⛵	Octavian's forces
⛵	Antony's and Cleopatra's forces
◄- -	Antony's and Cleopatra's attempted escape routes

her, leaving behind most of his remaining ships and men. It remains unclear whether these moves were part of the plan the two had worked out in advance. Plutarch and other ancient writers claimed that the lovers were cowards who abandoned their troops at the height of battle. But this charge was likely motivated by Roman hatred for Cleopatra and was circulated as part of Octavian's propaganda.

It is more probable that the lovers had planned their escape from the beginning (on the contingency that Antony could not achieve a quick victory) as part of an overall strategy for winning the war. In their view, losing a single battle was not catastrophic. They could use the riches of the East to regroup, build new fleets, and eventually overwhelm their enemy. Antony's abandonment of so many of his ships "can hardly be considered very noble," Ernle Bradford points out, "but it was practical. He had lost the battle of Actium . . . but he still had a chance to fight another day."[65]

This optimistic hope proved shortsighted, however. From a political and military standpoint, "another day" was not in the cards for Cleopatra and Antony. As they made their way southward toward Alexandria, they had not yet come face to face with what for them amounted to an awful truth—the outcome of the war, as well as their personal fates, had been decided by a single battle.

Chapter Seven

DEFIANT OPPONENT: CLEOPATRA'S CAPTURE AND DEATH

Actium proved to be a disaster from which Cleopatra and Antony were unable to recover. It is likely that at first they did not appreciate the true enormity of Octavian's and Agrippa's victory. It was not so much the number of ships and men the lovers lost since, in theory, these could be replaced. In fact, it is certain that Cleopatra and Antony planned to utilize Egypt's vast financial and other resources to build new fleets and launch fresh offensives. In the long run, Actium was more of a psychological victory for Octavian. In short, it made him look invincible and branded Cleopatra and her Roman companion as pathetic losers with no chance of survival, much less victory. As a result, they were unable to gather the support they needed to carry on the fight. Finally, they had to come to grips with the fact that their cause was lost and they themselves were doomed.

The Lovers' Power Base Collapses

The first indication that Cleopatra's and Antony's great military enterprise was in trouble occurred in the days immediately following the showdown at Actium. Antony's land army was still very much intact, and the soldiers were eager to fight for him. They were confused and disappointed, therefore, when he did not show up in their camp after the sea battle. Plutarch writes that they

longed to see him and were confident that he would appear from one quarter or another; indeed, such was their loyalty and courage that, even after his flight had become common knowledge, they still held together for seven days and ignored every approach made to them by Octavian.

Only after Antony's second in command, Canidius Crassus, abandoned the camp in the middle of the night did the troops find "themselves completely destitute, cut off from their supplies, and betrayed by their commanders."[66] Not surprisingly, they then surrendered and joined Octavian's army.

Antony and Cleopatra were understandably upset at the loss of their land army. But for a while they were sure they could raise all the fresh troops they needed. After all, the eastern sector of the Mediterranean world was by far the most populous, and nearly all of the leaders in the region had earlier pledged their support to them. According to Dio Cassius, Cleopatra and Antony "continued to make arrangements to carry on the war in Egypt both at sea and on land, and for this purpose they summoned all the neighboring tribes and rulers . . . to come to their help."[67]

To their dismay, however, the lovers rapidly discovered that the great power base they had built and thought was still broad and strong had collapsed. Now terrified of incurring Octavian's wrath, one local ruler after another refused to send troops, supplies, or any other form of support to Egypt. Typical was the reaction of Pinarius Scarpus, ruler of the neighboring kingdom of Cyrene. When he heard that Antony was approaching for an official visit, Dio later recalled,

Scarpus not only refused to receive him, but killed the delegation which Antony had sent ahead . . . and even executed some of the soldiers under his own command who had protested against this action. In consequence, Antony returned to Alexandria without having achieved anything.[68]

This famous statue of Octavian/Augustus was found at Prima Porta near Rome.

Meanwhile, Cleopatra encountered similar troubles farther to the east. She still had the sixty ships with which she had fled Actium as well as the vessels that had remained in Egypt when she was away in Greece. The ancient sources are not very clear about what she intended to do with these ships. But it looks as though she began transferring some of them to the Persian Gulf. Perhaps she planned to build a large new fleet there, where Octavian could not interfere. (When needed, this fleet could sail around the Arabian Peninsula and reach Egypt via the Red Sea.) Or maybe she planned to shift the theater of war to eastern Arabia in hopes of luring Octavian far from his power base and supply lines. Whatever her motivations may have been, this venture was foiled by an Arab chieftain, who burned the first contingent of ships the queen assembled in the gulf.

Appeals to Octavian

Not long after this setback, Cleopatra and Antony received even more bad news. Judaea's King Herod had abandoned them, proclaimed his support for Octavian, and transferred Antony's troops stationed in Judaea to the command of Octavian's officers. It was now clear that the lovers no longer had a credible way to oppose Julius Caesar's youthful but now extremely powerful heir.

At this point, Antony and Cleopatra initiated the only strategy left to them to keep themselves alive and her kingdom and their children's legacy intact. First, they tried to use their considerable riches to bribe Octavian. They also appealed to him to show them mercy for sentimental reasons. Dio writes:

> They dispatched emissaries to Octavian carrying peace proposals for him and bribes of money for his supporters. . . . Cleopatra promised to give him large sums of money, while Antony reminded him of their [former] friendship and their kinship by marriage. He also sought to defend his association with the Egyptian queen.[69]

In retrospect, Octavian's reactions to these overtures are fascinating and very revealing of his shrewd and practical character. In the long war of words leading up to Actium, he had publicly denounced Cleopatra as a witch and Antony as a slave to her spells, among many other insults. But privately, Octavian respected the talents of both of these adversaries. And he knew that, despite their resounding defeat and widespread loss of support, they still had the potential power to cause him considerable trouble and/or embarrassment. So he was willing to negotiate with Cleopatra behind the scenes in order to further his own aims. As suggested in several ancient accounts, it appears that he hoped to persuade her to ditch Antony. (This implies that Octavian assumed Cleopatra's relationship with Antony was mainly political and self-serving; he likely did not grasp the depth of her love for and loyalty to Antony, which made such betrayal out of the question.) Accordingly, Octavian replied to Cleopatra's offers with "a combination of threats and promises," Dio writes.

He was still afraid of several possible eventualities. The two [lovers] might despair of ever obtaining a pardon from him and so continue to resist. In that case they might [find some way to raise a new army and] either defeat him through their own efforts, or sail to Spain and Gaul [now France, and there build a new power base from which to attack Rome]. Alternately, they might destroy their wealth, which he was repeatedly informed was enormous. Cleopatra had . . . threatened to burn it all and herself with it if she failed to obtain the least of her demands. So Octavian sent [a negotiator] to charm her with a flow of fine words. . . . He also sent her a secret message that, if she would kill Antony, he would grant her a pardon and leave her kingdom untouched. . . . He hoped that by this approach . . . she might dispose of Antony and keep herself and her treasure unharmed.[70]

The Order of the Inseparable Death

Because Cleopatra refused to agree to Octavian's deal, the negotiations stalled. Now there was nothing left for the lovers but to sit and wait for the inevitable showdown

An early modern painting depicts the initial meeting between Octavian and the defeated Cleopatra. Little is known about the details of the encounter.

Shown is a Roman coin minted to celebrate Octavian's victory over Cleopatra.

with Octavian, for it was certain he would come after them sooner or later. True to her resilient character, Cleopatra found the inner resources to keep the government and court functioning and at least maintain the appearance that there was still hope for the country. According to Plutarch, she continued to socialize with friends and leading officials and to throw parties in the palace. At the same time, facing the inevitable in a practical way, she methodically began preparing her own tomb.

Meanwhile, Antony's initial reaction to their misfortunes was depression and withdrawal. This is perhaps understandable. After all, in a short span of time he had fallen from the heights of power and prestige to the depths of humiliation and rejection.

Perhaps even worse, most Romans now looked on him as a despicable traitor to his country. At first, he tried to kill himself. But the few officers and companions who still remained loyal to him stopped him. After that, as Plutarch tells it:

> Antony abandoned the city [Alexandria] and the company of his friends and went to live on the island of Pharos [on the northern edge of the main harbor] in a house which he had built on a jetty running into the sea. There he shut himself away from all human society, and said that . . . he distrusted and hated the whole human race.[71]

Cleopatra was not about to allow her lover and closest friend to spend his last days alone, however. After a while she managed to convince him to move back into the palace with her. Then, to cheer him up (according to Plutarch), she "plunged the city into a round of banquets, drinking parties, and lavish distributions of gifts." Gathering around them the friends they had partied with in happier days, they established an informal group they

called the Order of the Inseparable Death. Their friends joined it on the understanding that they would end their lives together, and they set themselves to charm away the days [that were left to them] with a succession of exquisite dinner parties.[72]

The Day of Reckoning

In the meantime, Octavian's spies kept him informed of these activities. Since his adversaries were for the moment effectively powerless, he did not hurry in launching the final offensive of the war and took the time to deal with some tax protests in Italy before setting sail for the East. It was not until July 30 B.C., therefore, that he arrived with his forces on Egypt's northern coast.

As the enemy approached Alexandria, Antony, who was at heart still a professional soldier who knew his duty, rose to the challenge. Doing his best to shake off the mood of despair and gloom that still gripped him, he bade Cleopatra farewell, gathered his few remaining loyal troops, and rode out to confront Octavian. The latter and his own troops were tired after their long trip and did not expect any significant resistance. So when Antony led his small band of cavalry in a daring charge on the enemy camp, he managed to create considerable confusion and afterward celebrated a minor victory.

Any hopes for overall victory were illusory, however. Cleopatra and Antony discovered this the hard way the next day, as Plutarch reports:

> As soon as it was light, Antony posted his infantry on the hills in front of the city and watched his ships as they put out and advanced against the enemy. Then, as he still believed that his fleet might carry the day, he stood and waited for the issue of the battle at sea. But his crews, as soon as they drew near the enemy, raised their oars in salute, and, when their greeting was returned, went over to Octavian. . . . No sooner had Antony witnessed this than he found himself abandoned by the cavalry, which likewise deserted to the enemy, and finally . . . he retreated into the city. [73]

In Octavian's Custody

As Octavian's soldiers entered Alexandria, the city erupted into a state of chaos. Thousands of people ran to and fro, some locking themselves inside their homes, others trying to get away into the countryside. It remains unclear how it happened, but Antony, who seems to have fled into the palace, heard an inaccurate report that Cleopatra was dead. In his view, she had been his last excuse to go on living, so he once more decided on suicide. "He stabbed himself with his own sword through the belly," Plutarch recalls, "and fell upon the bed." [74] The wound did not kill him right away, however. And as he lay there, writhing in agony, one of Cleopatra's attendants arrived and carried him out.

On the queen's orders, her servants bore Antony to her still unfinished tomb, in which she had barricaded herself along with most of her fabulous treasure. Plutarch later recorded the heart-rending scene that followed:

> [Cleopatra] showed herself at a window and let down cords and ropes to the ground. The slaves fastened Antony to these and the queen pulled him up with the help

Servants raise the mortally wounded Antony toward Cleopatra, who has locked herself in her tomb.

of her two waiting women, who were the only companions she had allowed to enter the monument with her. Those who were present say that there was never a more pitiable sight than the spectacle of Antony, covered with blood, struggling in his death agonies and stretching out his hands toward Cleopatra as he swung helplessly in the air. The task was almost beyond a woman's strength, and it was only with great difficulty that Cleopatra, clinging with both hands to the rope and with the muscles of her face distorted by the strain, was able to haul him up, while those on the ground encouraged her and shared her agony. When she had got him up and laid him upon a bed, she tore her dress and spread it over him, beat and lacerated her breasts, and smeared her face with the blood from his wounds. She called him her lord and husband and emperor and almost forgot her own misfortunes in her pity for his.[75]

After Antony died in Cleopatra's arms, she assessed her situation. Even in her grief, she retained the presence of mind to make one last ditch attempt to save her country, her throne, and her children's legacy. She could not be sure that Octavian would allow her to live. But perhaps her treasure was still a potent bargaining chip. "She therefore remained in seclusion within the building," Dio says,

> so that even if there was no other reason for keeping her alive, she could

at least trade upon Octavian's fear concerning her treasure to obtain a pardon and keep her throne. Even if she had to sink to such depths of misfortune, she remembered that she was queen and preferred to die bearing the title and majesty of a sovereign. . . . [Therefore] she kept a fire ready to destroy her treasure, and asps [poisonous snakes] and other reptiles [in case it became necessary] to end her life.[76]

Before the queen could either destroy the treasure or kill herself, however, Octavian's soldiers broke into the tomb and captured her. In the days that followed, the new master of the Roman world saw that she was treated well and allowed her to retain her servants and luxuries. Finally, these two giant legends—the most famous woman of ancient times and the future first (and arguably the greatest) Roman emperor—met face to face. For this fateful encounter, Dio writes,

> she prepared a superbly decorated apartment and a richly ornamented couch, dressed herself [in magnificent finery] and seated herself on the couch. Beside her she arranged many different portraits and busts of Julius Caesar, and in her bosom she carried all the letters Caesar had sent her.[77]

As Octavian entered the room, Cleopatra stood up and held her head high, displaying the pride and composure of a great ruler, which indeed she was. "Greetings, my lord," she told him, "for now the gods have given supremacy to you and taken it from me." [78]

In Death Unconquered

The meeting was cordial. The queen no doubt asked that her throne remain intact and that her children should receive their just inheritances. But her principal request seems to have been that, in case of her death, she be allowed to be buried beside her beloved Antony. As for Octavian, he assured his celebrated captive that he had no intention of killing her. There is little doubt that he was sincere about showing her a degree of mercy. According to Dio, he admired her. And we can speculate this was because of her cleverness, tenacity, and audaciousness, qualities he himself possessed in abundance. Octavian also worried that part of her treasure remained hidden and would never be found if he killed her. Finally, and perhaps most importantly, he wanted to take her back to Rome and march her in his triumph, as his adoptive father had done to her sister, Arsinoe.

Cleopatra had already anticipated the possibility that Octavian would take her to Rome and parade her in chains in public. Perhaps she would have willingly endured such humiliation if he had kept her son on the throne of a still independent Egypt (even if only as a puppet ruler beholden to Rome). But one of Octavian's officers, who had taken pity on the queen's plight, secretly told her that she and her children were to be placed on a ship bound for Rome three days hence.

Hearing this, the queen made up her mind to rob her enemy of his final victory over her by taking her own life. After locking herself in her tomb once again, along with her two trusted waiting women, Iras and Charmian, she poisoned herself. (One theory holds that the poison was administered by the bite of an asp; another claims that she pricked herself with a hairpin that had been dipped in poison.) At the last moment, Cleopatra sent a message to Octa-

---

Finding the Right Poison

Plutarch claimed (in his biography of Antony, quoted here from Makers of Rome*) that in preparation for her suicide Cleopatra tested various poisons to see which would be most effective and painless, an incident that, though possible, smacks of fable.*

Cleopatra collected together many kinds of deadly poisons and tested these on prisoners who had been condemned to death. . . . When she found out that the drugs which acted most quickly caused the victim to die in agony, while the milder poisons were slow to take effect, she went on to examine the lethal qualities of various venomous creatures. . . . After trying almost every possibility, she discovered that it was the bite of the asp alone which brought on a kind of drowsy lethargy and numbness . . . while the senses were gradually dulled.

In a scene envisioned by a modern artist, Cleopatra tests various poisons by trying them on prisoners. This incident is most likely fanciful.

vian, informing him that she had chosen death rather than remain alive in his captivity. Startled and concerned, he sent soldiers to stop her.

However, as the shrewd queen had anticipated would happen, these men were too late. In one of the most renowned passages of ancient literature, Plutarch describes what they found inside the tomb:

> When they opened the doors, they found Cleopatra lying dead upon a golden couch dressed in her royal robes. Of her two women, Iras lay dying at her feet, while Charmian, already tottering and scarcely able to hold up her head, was arranging the crown which encircled her mistress's brow. Then one of the guards cried out angrily, "Charmian, is this well done?" And she answered, "It is well done, and fitting for a princess descended of so many royal kings," and, as she uttered the words, she fell dead by the side of the couch.[79]

Cleopatra was thirty-nine years old when she took her life. She had ruled Ptolemaic Egypt for twenty-one of those years, during which she had shown herself to be the equal in political skills, courage, and boldness to the three most powerful men in her world.

Cleopatra was already dead when Octavian's men entered her tomb. By killing herself, she deftly thwarted his plans to bring her in chains to Rome.

Indeed, she had shared her bed with and given her complete allegiance and trust to two of these men. In this regard, Dio later tried to sum up her legacy this way: "Through her own unaided genius she captivated two of the greatest Romans of her time, and because of the third, she destroyed herself." [80]

Yet posterity has shown that on that fateful day it was only Cleopatra's mortal body that was destroyed, a fate that befalls everyone in the end. The memory of her extraor-dinary personality, deeds, and capacity for love endured. It outlived Octavian and his heirs; it outlived Rome itself and the medieval kingdoms that replaced it; and it remains as alive and vivid today as it was on the day of her passing. Surely it is no exaggeration to say, therefore, that, in spite of the loss of her treasures, her kingdom, and her very life, in death this extraordinary woman was, and will always remain, unconquered.

ENDURING LEGEND: CLEOPATRA IN LITERATURE AND ART

All through her reign, but especially in its final moments, Cleopatra worried about the fate of her kingdom, her children's future, and her own legacy. All of these ended up in Roman hands. Rome absorbed Egypt into its growing empire, extinguishing the long line of pharaohs, a tradition stretching back thirty centuries. And Cleopatra's children met either death or obscurity. The Romans would have liked to erase the memory of the audacious queen herself, this woman "whose charms brought scandal on the Roman arms,"[81] as the Roman poet Propertius put it. But this they could not do. In fact, their strenuous attempt to blacken her name only perpetuated it and immortalized her character and deeds. This proved to be the first of many rounds of mythmaking that have made her one of history's greatest legendary and romantic figures.

A Mix of Generosity and Ruthlessness

Immortalizing Cleopatra was certainly not Octavian's intent in the weeks, months, and years following her defeat and death. For him, dealing with her remains, her offspring, and her kingdom was only a small part of his overall consolidation of power over the known world. The demise of Cleopatra and Antony removed the last obstacle that stood between Octavian and ultimate power. The last remaining triumvir now commanded all of Rome's armies and held the riches of Egypt and the rest of the East in his hands. In the three years following his victory at Actium, he quietly amassed a wide array of powers that gave him almost total control over the now-defunct Republic. Even the Senate, once the chief organ of Rome's government, was

By tradition, emperors everywhere have ruled with a mix of generosity and ruthlessness, of mercy and vengeance. Augustus was no different, including the way he (while still called Octavian) handled the aftermath of Cleopatra's fall. On the one hand, he kept his promise to bury her with her beloved Antony. Though "vexed at Cleopatra's death," Plutarch writes, Octavian "could not but admire the nobility of her spirit, and he gave orders that she should be buried with royal splendor and magnificence, and her body laid beside Antony's."[82] The victor of Actium also showed mercy to Cleopatra's and Antony's children. Alexander Helios, Cleopatra Selene, and Ptolemy Philadelphus were not only spared but in one of the truly noblest gestures in the historical annals, his sister Octavia, whom Antony had treated so shabbily, raised and educated them.

Less fortunate were Cleopatra's and Antony's other children, as well as the Egyptian people, who all became the victims of the ruthless side of Octavian's character. As heir to the name, honors, fortune, and political legacy of the great Caesar, Octavian did not want to risk a potential future challenge by Caesarion, who was Caesar's real, rather than adopted, son. So the boy was promptly executed. Octavian also coldly eliminated Antyl-

A vase painting from about 1760 shows a portly Cleopatra preparing to die.

overshadowed. Bowing to the inevitable, in 27 B.C. its members bestowed on Caesar's heir the name of Augustus, "the revered one." And though the recipient of this honor never called himself an emperor, he was in fact the first in a long line of them.

Noted English sculptor Henry Weekes created this statue of Cleopatra.

lus, Antony's son by Fulvia, to ensure that no challenge could ever come from the male heir of a former triumvir. As for Egypt, Octavian annexed it outright, ending its long history as an independent nation. For centuries to come, the fate of the average Egyptian would be decided in faraway Rome.

Lustful Prostitute or Brave Queen?

One thing that later generations of Egyptians could look back on with pride was the memory of their last pharaoh, Cleopatra, who had bravely stood up to the Romans. This, of course, was the polar opposite of the way the average Roman viewed her and her memory. Almost to a man, Roman poets and other writers vilified her. Dio called her "a woman of insatiable sexuality and . . . avarice [greed]."[83] Horace claimed she "was preparing the ruin of our city [Rome] and the funeral of our empire."[84] And the poet Lucan railed against "Cleopatra, the shame of Egypt, the lascivious [lustful] fury who was to become the bane of Rome."[85] Dio Cassius, Suetonius, Plutarch, and others recorded the major events of the famous queen's rise and fall, yet they freely mixed rumors and propaganda with the facts. As a result, by the time that Rome disintegrated in the fifth and sixth centuries A.D., her true character and many of her accomplishments were already distorted in a romanticized haze.

Moreover, in the centuries that followed, Cleopatra's legend continued to grow. A tenth-century Arab historian, Al Masudi, ascribed numerous books of medicine and science to her that she almost certainly did not write. Meanwhile, the leading medieval European poets saw her larger-than-life image as rich material for their pens. And their embellishments and outright fabrications only made that image even larger. Some, like Roman writers before them, were highly critical. In his *Concerning Famous Women*, for example, the Italian master Giovanni Boccaccio (born 1313) said that she was a

> prostitute of Oriental [Eastern, but at the time also meaning corrupt] kings, and greedy for gold and jewels. She not only stripped her lovers of these things with her [seductive] art, but it was also said that she emptied the temples and the sacred places of the Egyptians of their vases, statues, and other treasures. . . . [Later] she went to meet [Antony] and easily ensnared that lustful man with her beauty and wanton eyes. She kept him wretchedly in love with her . . . [and] as the insatiable woman's craving for kingdoms grew day by day, to grasp everything at once she asked Antony for the Roman empire.[86]

In contrast, the English poet Geoffrey Chaucer, author of the *Canterbury Tales*, saw some good qualities in the famous queen. In particular, he emphasized her and Antony's capacity for romantic love, and he did so in a manner in keeping with popular medieval tales of bold knights and their fair damsels who nobly risked all for each other. "His love for Cleopatra was so great," Chaucer writes of Antony,

> that the whole world he valued not at all. . . . He had no fear of fighting or of dying to keep her safe and maintain her right. And she, the queen, in turn adored this knight, for his great worth and for his chivalry. . . . This Cleopatra suffered for his sake with sorrows such that no tongue could narrate. . . . [After his death she proclaimed,] "Beloved, whom my heart always obeyed . . . to myself I made a promise . . . that all of your feelings, good or bad, I'd share. . . . What you felt, I'd feel also, life or death; and this same covenant [agreement] . . . I will fulfill [now]; and then this shall be seen: there never lived and loved a truer queen." And with that word . . . this woman brave leaped down among the serpents in the grave.[87]

Cleopatra on the Stage

Another literary genre that embraced Cleopatra was drama, as many playwrights in Europe's Renaissance and early modern era told her story. All contributed to the ongoing idealization and/or defamation of her character and featured romantic and colorful imagery, most of it completely fabricated. In his *Antony and Cleopatra*, for example, the sixteenth-century Italian Don

This painting of Cleopatra emphasizes her seductive qualities. Her features in this work resemble those from ancient coins.

Celso Pitorelli had Antony dream about Cleopatra turning into a snake and enveloping him in her coils.

The most famous plays about Cleopatra were written by Englishmen—William Shakespeare (*Antony and Cleopatra*, 1607) and George Bernard Shaw (*Caesar and Cleopatra*, 1900). Shakespeare based his version mainly on Plutarch's *Life of Antony*. As a result, the play retains that ancient writer's negative biases and preconceptions about Cleopatra. At one point, Octavian's character says that Antony has "given his empire up to a whore." Octavian also calls Cleopatra's and Antony's children "the unlawful issue that their lust . . . hath made between them."[88] Yet, like Chaucer, Shakespeare also plays up the great love between the title characters, emphasizing that, greedy and lustful or not, she truly loved

arrived in Egypt, and fearing them, she hides atop a stone sphinx in the desert. There, by chance, in a romantic moonlit setting, Julius Caesar himself finds her. Not realizing who he is, she warns, "Climb up here, quickly; or the Romans will come and eat you." After she introduces herself, Caesar asks, "Are you afraid of the Romans?" and the following delightful exchange ensues:

CLEOPATRA: Oh, they would eat us if they caught us. They are barbarians. Their chief is called Julius Caesar. His father was a tiger and his mother a burning mountain; and his nose is like an elephant's trunk. They all have long noses, and ivory tusks, and little tails, and seven arms with a hundred arrows in each; and they live on human flesh.

CAESAR: Would you like me to show you a real Roman?

CLEOPATRA: No. You are frightening me. . . .

CAESAR: Cleopatra, can you see my face well?

CLEOPATRA: Yes, it is so white in the moonlight.

CAESAR: Are you sure it is the

Antony and would gladly die for him. Her death scene is a masterpiece of romantic longing for a lost lover.

Written nearly three centuries later, Shaw's play is more lighthearted and whimsical, though no less penetrating and entertaining. His Cleopatra, a product more of his imagination than the ancient sources, is a charming but frightened young woman who has recently been thrown out of the palace (by Ptolemy and Pothinus). Hearing that the Romans have

moonlight that makes me look whiter than an Egyptian? Do you notice that I have a rather long nose? . . . It is a Roman nose, Cleopatra.[89]

As the rest of the play unfolds, Caesar helps the naive young woman transform herself into a strong and capable ruler.

Immortality Through Art

Cleopatra's legend and mystique have fascinated artists of all kinds no less than writers over the centuries. The Italian Renaissance master Michelangelo painted her with serpents in her hair and wrapped around her body; and a later Italian artist, Alessandro Turchi made her grief-stricken pose over the dead Antony look like traditional depictions of Mary lamenting for the crucified Jesus. Among others, the nineteenth-century French painter Jean Gérôme chose to re-create scenes from the works of Plutarch and other ancient writers. His famous painting of the Egyptian queen shows her confronting Caesar after smuggling herself into the palace.

Highly romanticized versions of Cleopatra's story have also been produced by composers. One of the greatest musical versions of that story remains George Frideric Handel's opera *Julius Caesar*, written in 1724. Caesar is portrayed in the piece as a supremely heroic figure and Cleopatra as his exotic love interest. Other notable musical renditions of Cleopatra's legend include an 1806 opera by Italian composer Antonio Sografi; a long romantic song by nineteenth-century French composer Hector Berlioz; and British composer John Scott's haunting film score to the 1972 movie version of Shakespeare's *Antony and Cleopatra*.

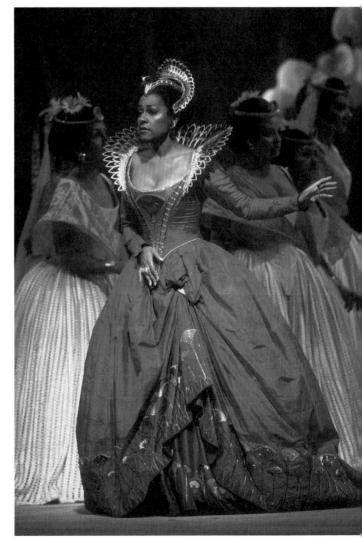

Noted soprano Kathleen Battle plays Cleopatra in a modern production of Handel's opera Julius Caesar.

The latter has been only one of many films featuring Cleopatra's character. In fact, she has proved to be one of the most popular and recurring historical figures in the history of the movies. At least six silent films were made about her before 1930, perhaps the most famous and successful being the 1917 version starring Theda Bara in the title role, Fritz Leiber as Caesar, and Thurston Hall as Antony. The first big sound version was director Cecil B. DeMille's 1934 epic, which received an Oscar nomination for best picture. Claudette Colbert portrayed Cleopatra, Warren William was Caesar, and Henry Wilcoxon played Antony. Other notable versions included the 1946 film based on Shaw's play, with Vivien Leigh (who played Scarlet O'Hara in *Gone with the Wind*) as Cleopatra and Claude Rains as Caesar; the 1972 version of *Antony and Cleopatra*, directed by and starring (as Antony) Charlton Heston; and a 1999 made-for-television movie based on Margaret George's book, *The Memoirs of Cleopatra*.

By far the most famous and spectacular of all the Cleopatra films, however, was the mammoth 1963 epic *Cleopatra*, directed by Joseph L. Mankiewicz. The stars were Elizabeth Taylor in the title role, Richard Burton as Antony, Rex Harrison as Caesar, and Roddy McDowall as Octavian. The most expensive film ever made up to that time (at the then-staggering cost of $62 million), it is a long, somewhat slow-moving, but visually exquisite work that stays true to Plutarch and other ancient sources most of the time. In a way, it remains the ultimate expression of the Cleopatra legend because it brings together all the major literary and artistic genres (writing, painting, architecture, costume design, music, photography, acting, and directing) in one powerful, highly memorable statement.

Many more movies, books, plays, paintings, and musical pieces will surely depict Cleopatra in the decades and centuries to come. Truly a woman for the ages, she will likely continue to fascinate people in each new generation. Every now and then a human being achieves such extraordinary accomplishments and/or stature that he or she is remembered by nearly everyone ever after. Among these immortals are Alexander the Great, Julius Caesar, Joan of Arc, Isaac Newton, Napoléon Bonaparte, Ludwig van Beethoven, and Mahatma Gandhi. Cleopatra VII, Egypt's tragic yet eternally inspiring last pharaoh, is another.

Notes

Introduction:
The Distorting Mirrors of Cleopatra's Reflection

1. Peter Green, *Alexander to Actium: The Historical Evolution of the Hellenistic Age.* Berkeley and Los Angeles: University of California Press, 1990, p. 682.
2. Lucy Hughes-Hallett, *Cleopatra: Histories, Dreams, and Distortions.* New York: HarperCollins, 1991, p. 1.
3. Théophile Gautier, *One of Cleopatra's Nights*, trans. Lacfadio Hearn. New York: Worthington, 1882, p. 8.
4. Horace, "Cleopatra," trans. Barklie Henry, in *The Latin Poets*, ed. Francis R.B. Godolphin. New York: Random House, 1949, p. 343.
5. Hughes-Hallett, *Cleopatra*, p. 5.
6. Quoted in Dio Cassius, *Roman History*, excerpted in *The Roman History: The Reign of Augustus*, trans. Ian Scott-Kilvert. New York: Penguin, 1987, pp. 52–53.
7. Hughes-Hallett, *Cleopatra*, p. 2.

Chapter 1:
Child of Privilege: The World of Cleopatra's Youth

8. Theocritus, *Idylls*, in Naphtali Lewis, *Greeks in Ptolemaic Egypt.* Oxford, UK: Clarendon, 1986, p. 11.
9. Chester G. Starr, *A History of the Ancient World.* New York: Oxford University Press, 1991, p. 408.
10. Lewis, *Greeks in Ptolemaic Egypt*, pp. 154–55.
11. Michael Foss, *The Search for Cleopatra.* London: Michael O'Mara, 1997, p. 49.
12. Strabo, *Geography*, trans. Horace L. Jones. Cambridge, MA: Harvard University Press, 1967, pp. 69, 71.
13. Ernle Bradford, *Cleopatra.* New York: Harcourt, Brace, Jovanovich, 1972, p. 37.

Chapter 2:
Lover and Ally: Cleopatra and Julius Caesar

14. Julius Caesar, *Commentary on the Civil Wars*, published as *Caesar: The Civil War*, trans. John Carter. New York: Oxford University press, 1997, p. 133.
15. Appian, *The Civil Wars*, trans. John Carter. New York: Penguin, 1996, p. 114.
16. Plutarch, *Life of Caesar*, in *Fall of the Roman Republic: Six Lives by Plutarch*, trans. Rex Warner. New York: Penguin, 1972, p. 290.

17. Plutarch, *Caesar*, p. 290.
18. Plutarch, *Caesar*, p. 290.
19. Foss, *Search for Cleopatra*, pp. 79–80.
20. Caesar, *Commentary*, p. 136.
21. Caesar, *Commentary*, p. 137.
22. Caesar, *Commentary*, p. 138.
23. *The Alexandrian War* (author unknown, but ostensibly Aulus Hirtius), in Carter, *Caesar*, p. 147.
24. Appian, *Civil Wars*, p. 117.
25. Suetonius, *Lives of the Twelve Caesars*, published as *The Twelve Caesars*, trans. Robert Graves, rev. Michael Grant. New York: Penguin, 1979, p. 36.
26. Cicero, *Letters to Atticus*, vol. 4, trans. E.O. Winstedt. Cambridge, MA: Harvard University Press, 1961, pp. 257, 259.

Chapter 3:
Lover and Ally Again: Cleopatra and Mark Antony

27. Appian, *Civil Wars*, p. 272.
28. Plutarch, *Life of Antony*, in *Makers of Rome: Nine Lives by Plutarch*, trans. Ian Scott-Kilvert. New York: Penguin, 1965, pp. 292–93.
29. Plutarch, *Life of Antony*, p. 293.
30. Plutarch, *Life of Antony*, p. 293.
31. Plutarch, *Life of Antony*, p. 294.
32. Plutarch, *Life of Antony*, p. 295.
33. Plutarch, *Life of Antony*, pp. 296–97.
34. Plutarch, *Life of Antony*, p. 297.

Chapter 4:
Efficient, Shrewd, and Rich: Cleopatra as a Ruler

35. Seneca, *Natural Questions*, vol. 2, trans. T.H. Corcoran. Cambridge, MA: Harvard University Press, 1972, p. 33.
36. Quoted in Jack Lindsay, *Cleopatra*. London: Constable, 1970, pp. 127–28.
37. M.I. Finley, *The Ancient Economy*. Berkeley and Los Angeles: University of California Press, 1985, pp. 22, 26.
38. Josephus, *The Jewish War*, trans. G.A. Williamson, rev. E. Mary Smallwood. New York: Penguin, 1981, p. 75.
39. These obelisks were not raised until after Cleopatra's death, but they came to be associated with her anyway, partly because she had begun the building and also because people in later ages assumed, incorrectly, that she had built most or all of the great monuments in Alexandria. In the late 1800s one of the two obelisks was transported to London and the other to New York. Both still stand and continue to delight tourists.
40. Philo, *Embassy to Gaius*, quoted in Jean-Yves Empereur, *Alexandria Rediscovered*. New York: George Braziller, 1998, pp. 112–13.
41. Quoted in Athenaeus, *Sophists at Dinner*, vol. 4, trans. Charles B. Gulick. Cambridge, MA: Harvard University Press, 1928, p. 147.

Chapter 5:
Master Propagandist: Cleopatra Molds Her Own Image

42. Hughes-Hallett, *Cleopatra*, pp. 75–76.
43. Hughes-Hallett, *Cleopatra*, p. 17.
44. Susan Walker, "Cleopatra's Images: Reflections of Reality," in *Cleopatra of Egypt: From History to Myth*, ed. Susan Walker and Peter Higgs. Princeton, NJ: Princeton University Press, 2001, p. 143.
45. Bradford, *Cleopatra*, p. 12.
46. Herodotus, *The Histories*, trans. Aubrey de Sélincourt. New York: Penguin, 1972, p. 143.
47. Apuleius, *The Golden Ass*, trans. P.G. Walsh. Oxford, UK: Oxford University Press, 1994, pp. 219–20.
48. Plutarch, *Life of Antony*, p. 322.
49. Foss, *The Search for Cleopatra*, pp. 105–106.
50. Hughes-Hallett, *Cleopatra*, p. 75.

Chapter 6:
Challenger of Rome: Cleopatra Versus Octavian

51. Plutarch, *Life of Antony*, p. 303.
52. Plutarch, *Life of Antony*, p. 326.
53. Dio Cassius, *Roman History*, pp. 38–39.
54. Plutarch, *Life of Antony*, pp. 321–22.
55. Plutarch, *Life of Antony*, p. 322.
56. Dio Cassius, *Roman History*, p. 38.
57. Virgil, *Fourth Eclogue*, in *The Poems of Virgil*, James Rhoades, trans. Chicago: Encyclopaedia Britannica, 1952, p. 14.
58. Plutarch, *Life of Antony*, p. 324.
59. Plutarch, *Life of Antony*, p. 329.
60. Plutarch, *Life of Antony*, p. 330.
61. Quoted in Dio Cassius, *Roman History*, p. 54.
62. Dio Cassius, *Roman History*, pp. 57–58.
63. Dio Cassius, *Roman History*, p. 59.
64. Plutarch, *Life of Antony*, p. 331.
65. Bradford, *Cleopatra*, p. 237.

Chapter 7:
Defiant Opponent: Cleopatra's Capture and Death

66. Plutarch, *Life of Antony*, p. 334.
67. Dio Cassius, *Roman History*, pp. 67–68.
68. Dio Cassius, *Roman History*, p. 67.
69. Dio Cassius, *Roman History*, pp. 68–69.
70. Dio Cassius, *Roman History*, pp. 69–70.
71. Plutarch, *Life of Antony*, p. 335.
72. Plutarch, *Life of Antony*, p. 337.
73. Plutarch, *Life of Antony*, p. 340.
74. Plutarch, *Life of Antony*, p. 341.
75. Plutarch, *Life of Antony*, pp. 341–42.
76. Dio Cassius, *Roman History*, p. 72.
77. Dio Cassius, *Roman History*, p. 73.
78. Quoted in Dio Cassius, *Roman History*, p. 73.
79. Plutarch, *Life of Antony*, p. 347.
80. Dio Cassius, *Roman History*, p. 76.

Epilogue:
Enduring Legend: Cleopatra in Literature and Art

81. Propertius, "Cleopatra and Caesar," trans. Seymour G. Tremenheere, in Godolphin, *Latin Poets*, p. 368.
82. Plutarch, *Life of Antony*, p. 348.
83. Dio Cassius, *Roman History*, p. 76.
84. Horace, "Cleopatra," in Godolphin, *Latin Poets*, p. 243.
85. Lucan, *Pharsalia*, quoted in *Cleopatra: The Life and Death of a Pharaoh*, by Edith Flamarion. New York: Harry N. Abrams, 1997, p. 115.
86. Giovanni Boccaccio, *Concerning Famous Women*, trans. Guido A. Guarino. London: Allen and Unwin, 1964, pp. 82–83.
87. Geoffrey Chaucer, "The Legend of Cleopatra," in *The Legend of Good Women*, trans. Ann McMillan. Houston: Rice University Press, 1987, pp. 83, 86.
88. William Shakespeare, *Antony and Cleopatra*, ed. Maynard Mack. Baltimore: Penguin, 1960, act 3, scene 6, lines 66–67 and 7–8.
89. George Bernard Shaw, *Caesar and Cleopatra*. Baltimore: Penguin, 1966, pp. 29–30.

Chronology

B.C.

332
Greek conqueror Alexander the Great liberates Egypt from Persian control and soon afterward establishes the city of Alexandria in the Nile Delta.

323
Alexander dies, leaving his leading generals to fight over his empire.

305
Alexander's former general, Ptolemy, declares himself king of Egypt, initiating Egypt's royal Ptolemaic dynasty.

100
Julius Caesar, the Roman aristocrat who will one day conquer the Mediterranean world and have a son with Cleopatra, is born.

ca. 83
Marcus Antonius (Mark Antony), the Roman army officer who will later become Caesar's supporter and Cleopatra's lover and ally, is born.

80
Ptolemy XII Auletes ascends Egypt's throne.

69
Cleopatra VII, daughter of Auletes, is born.

63
Octavius Caesar (Octavian), later Caesar's adopted son and later still, Augustus, the first Roman emperor, is born.

60
Caesar, the noted general Pompey, and the wealthy businessman Crassus form a ruling coalition that later becomes known as the First Triumvirate.

57
Auletes travels to Rome to gain the support of Roman notables.

51
Auletes dies, leaving his throne to Cleopatra, now eighteen, and her younger brother, Ptolemy XIII, and intending for them to rule jointly.

49
At the urgings of his regent and other ambitious courtiers, Ptolemy drives Cleopatra away and she takes refuge in Syria; with Crassus dead and the triumvirate in shambles, a Roman civil war erupts, pitting Caesar against Pompey.

48
Caesar defeats Pompey at Pharsalus (in Greece); Pompey flees to Egypt, where Ptolemy has him murdered; Caesar arrives, forms an alliance with Cleopatra, and backs her in a local civil war against her brother.

47

Caesar defeats Ptolemy and his advisers and reinstalls Cleopatra on the Egyptian throne; Caesar returns to Rome; later that year, his and Cleopatra's son, Caesarion (Ptolemy XV), is born.

44

Cleopatra, accompanied by Caesarion, visits Caesar in Rome; on March 15 Caesar is stabbed to death in the Senate House by a group of disgruntled legislators who hope to restore the power and dignity of the disintegrating Roman Republic; Caesar's leading assassins flee to Greece as his friend and supporter, Mark Antony, emerges as his possible successor.

43

Antony, Octavian, and a powerful general named Lepidus form the Second Triumvirate and murder many of their political opponents.

42

Antony and Octavian defeat Caesar's assassins at Philippi (in Greece).

41

Antony, now the leading triumvir, summons Cleopatra to his headquarters at Tarsus (in Asia Minor); the two become lovers and allies.

40

Antony and Octavian sign a treaty of mutual support; Antony marries Octavian's sister, Octavia; Cleopatra gives birth to twins by Antony—Alexander Helios and Cleopatra Selene.

37

Antony sends Octavia back to Italy and rejoins Cleopatra.

36

Antony's military expedition against the Near Eastern realm of Parthia is unsuccessful; he and Cleopatra have another child—Ptolemy Philadelphus; Octavian removes Lepidus from the triumvirate and puts him under permanent house arrest.

34

In a lavish ceremony known as the Donations of Alexandria, Antony grants several eastern lands and royal titles to Cleopatra and their children, raising the ire of Octavian and most Romans.

33–32

Octavian engages in a heated propaganda war with Antony and Cleopatra, suggesting that Antony has lost his wits and Cleopatra wants to become queen of Rome; Antony divorces Octavia; Octavian declares war on Cleopatra.

31

Octavian and his talented commander, Marcus Agrippa, defeat Antony and Cleopatra at Actium (in western Greece); the lovers flee to Alexandria.

30

Octavian pursues his adversaries to Egypt; Antony and Cleopatra commit suicide; Octavian has Caesarion killed; Octavian annexes Egypt as a Roman province.

27

The now powerless Roman Senate confers on Octavian, who has emerged as the most powerful man in the known world, the title of Augustus, "the revered one;" modern historians mark this event as the beginning of the Roman Empire.

For Further Reading

Books

Alice C. Desmond, *Cleopatra's Children.* New York: Dodd, Mead, 1971. A very informative and interesting book that begins with a general sketch of Cleopatra's life, then explores the fates of her children, especially Cleopatra Selene.

Bruce Field, *Cleopatra in the Night: And Other Poems.* McKinleyville, CA: Fithian, 1999. An excellent collection of entertaining and thought-provoking verses based on Cleopatra's life and legend.

Laura Foreman, *Cleopatra's Palace: In Search of a Legend.* New York: Discovery Communications, 1999. A colorful, well-illustrated book about the quest to recover artifacts from sections of ancient Alexandria that are now submerged under water.

Don Nardo, *Julius Caesar.* San Diego: Lucent, 1997. A fast-paced biography that fills out the details of Caesar's life and exploits both before and after he met Cleopatra.

———, *Women of Ancient Greece.* San Diego: Lucent, 2000. This book provides a larger context for Cleopatra's political and cultural achievements in what was essentially a man's world in which a woman of intelligence and achievement was considered a threat to the established order.

George Bernard Shaw, *Caesar and Cleopatra.* Baltimore: Penguin, 1966. Shaw's wonderful, witty version of the relationship between these two immortals remains first-rate entertainment for people of all ages and backgrounds.

Web Sites

Cleopatra (Film Guide) (www.historyinfilm.com/cleo/cleohome.htm). A well-organized examination of the famous 1963 film version of Cleopatra's exploits, with numerous links to various aspects of the movie and its educational value.

Cleopatra VII, Ptolemaic Dynasty (www.touregypt.net/cleopatr.htm). A useful general overview of Cleopatra's life and exploits.

Cleopatra's Images on Coins (http://sangha.net/messengers/cleopatra/coins.htm). An excellent site that displays close-up views of ancient coins bearing portraits of Cleopatra and Mark Antony.

Works Consulted

Major Works

Ernle Bradford, *Cleopatra*. New York: Harcourt, Brace, Jovanovich, 1972. A well-written overview of the famous queen that emphasizes her political exploits, along with those of her allies and opponents.

John M. Carter, *The Battle of Actium*. London: Hamish Hamilton, 1970. This commendable volume traces the events leading up to the famous sea battle as well as the known facts about the battle itself.

Edith Flamarion, *Cleopatra: The Life and Death of a Pharaoh*. New York: Harry N. Abrams, 1997. A general synopsis of Cleopatra's life and legend, featuring numerous complete and partial primary source quotations.

Michael Foss, *The Search for Cleopatra*. London: Michael O'Mara, 1997. A very engaging and at times thought-provoking brief overview of Cleopatra's life and exploits.

Michael Grant, *Caesar*. London: Weidenfeld and Nicolson, 1974. An excellent summary of the life and deeds of the great Roman politician and military general, with a nice overview of his relationship with Cleopatra.

———, *Cleopatra*. New York: Simon and Schuster, 1972. One of the leading scholarly works on the renowned Egyptian queen and a must for those studying her in detail.

Peter Green, *Alexander to Actium: The Historical Evolution of the Hellenistic Age*. Berkeley and Los Angeles: University of California Press, 1990. The definitive work on the Hellenistic Age, of which Cleopatra's struggle with Rome formed the final major episode.

Mary Hamer, *Signs of Cleopatra: History, Politics, Representation*. London: Routledge, 1993. A scholarly look at the evolution of Cleopatra's image as a ruler and person.

Lucy Hughes-Hallett, *Cleopatra: Histories, Dreams, and Distortions*. New York: HarperCollins, 1991. This important and thoroughly entertaining (but sophisticated and complex) volume examines the development of Cleopatra's mystique from ancient times to the present.

Elenor G. Huzar, *Mark Antony: A Biography*. Minneapolis: University of Minnesota Press, 1978. Contains everything you ever wanted to know about this Roman notable who became Cleopatra's ally and lover.

Jack Lindsay, *Cleopatra*. London: Constable, 1970. One of the major works about Cleopatra—long, detailed, and written by a fine, reliable scholar.

Jon Solomon, *The Ancient World in the*

Cinema. New Haven, CT: Yale University Press, 2001. An excellent synopsis and analysis of films about ancient times, including all of the movies depicting Cleopatra's story.

Susan Walker and Peter Higgs, eds., *Cleopatra of Egypt: From History to Myth.* Princeton, NJ: Princeton University Press, 2001. A very useful compilation of data about various ancient artifacts relating to Cleopatra, her struggle, and her era.

Other Important Works

Primary Sources

Appian, *The Civil Wars.* Trans. John Carter. New York: Penguin, 1996.

Apuleius, *The Golden Ass.* Trans. P.G. Walsh. Oxford, UK: Oxford University Press, 1994.

Arrian, *Anabasis Alexandri*, published as *The Campaigns of Alexander.* Trans. Aubrey de Sélincourt. New York: Penguin, 1971.

Athenaeus, *Sophists at Dinner.* Vol. 4. Trans. Charles B. Gulick. Cambridge, MA: Harvard University Press, 1928.

Giovanni Boccaccio, *Concerning Famous Women.* Trans. Guido A. Guarino. London: Allen and Unwin, 1964.

Julius Caesar, *Commentary on the Civil Wars*, published as *Caesar: The Civil War.* Trans. John Carter. New York: Oxford University Press, 1997.

Geoffrey Chaucer, *The Legend of Good Women.* Trans. Ann McMillan. Houston: Rice University Press, 1987.

Cicero, *Letters to Atticus.* Vol. 4. Trans. E.O. Winstedt. Cambridge, MA: Harvard University Press, 1961.

Dio Cassius, *Roman History*, excerpted in *The Roman History: The Reign of Augustus.* Trans. Ian Scott-Kilvert. New York: Penguin, 1987.

Diodorus Siculus, *Library of History.* 12 vols. Various trans. Cambridge, MA: Harvard University Press, 1962–1967.

Herodotus, *The Histories.* Trans. Aubrey de Sélincourt. New York: Penguin, 1972.

Francis R.B. Godolphin, ed., *The Latin Poets.* New York: Random House, 1949.

Josephus, *The Jewish War.* Trans. G.A. Williamson. Rev. E. Mary Smallwood. New York: Penguin, 1981.

Pliny the Elder, *Natural History*, excerpted in *Natural History: A Selection.* Trans. John F. Healy. New York: Penguin, 1991.

Plutarch, *Parallel Lives*, excerpted in *Fall of the Roman Republic: Six Lives by Plutarch.* Trans. Rex Warner. New York: Penguin, 1972; also excerpted in *Makers of Rome: Nine Lives by Plutarch.* Trans. Ian Scott-Kilvert. New York: Penguin, 1965; and *The Age of Alexander: Nine Greek Lives by Plutarch.* Trans. Ian Scott-Kilvert. New York: Penguin, 1973.

James Rhoades, trans., *The Poems of Virgil.* Chicago: Encyclopaedia Britannica, 1952.

Seneca, *Natural Questions.* Vol. 2. Trans. T.H. Corcoran. Cambridge, MA: Harvard University Press, 1972.

Strabo, *Geography.* Trans. Horace L. Jones. Cambridge, MA: Harvard University Press, 1967.

Suetonius, *Lives of the Twelve Caesars*, published as *The Twelve Caesars*. Trans. Robert Graves. Rev. Michael Grant. New York: Penguin, 1979.

Modern Sources

F.R. Cowell, *Cicero and the Roman Republic.* Baltimore: Penguin, 1967.

Michael Crawford, *The Roman Republic.* Cambridge, MA: Harvard University Press, 1992.

Jean-Yves Empereur, *Alexandria Rediscovered.* New York: George Braziller, 1998.

M.I. Finley, *The Ancient Economy.* Berkeley and Los Angeles: University of California Press, 1985.

J.F.C. Fuller, *Julius Caesar: Man, Soldier, and Tyrant.* New Brunswick, NJ: Rutgers University Press, 1965.

Théophile Gautier, *One of Cleopatra's Nights.* Trans. Lacfadio Hearn. New York: Worthington, 1882.

Michael Grant, *From Alexander to Cleopatra: The Hellenistic World.* New York: Charles Scribner's Sons, 1982.

———, *History of Rome.* New York: Scribner's, 1978.

Naphtali Lewis, *Greeks in Ptolemaic Egypt.* Oxford, UK: Clarendon, 1986.

William L. Rodgers, *Greek and Roman Naval Warfare.* Annapolis, MD: Naval Institute, 1964.

William Shakespeare, *Antony and Cleopatra.* Ed. Maynard Mack. Baltimore: Penguin, 1960. (One of dozens of comparable editions available.)

Chester G. Starr, *A History of the Ancient World.* New York: Oxford University Press, 1991.

Lily Ross Taylor, *Party Politics in the Age of Caesar.* Berkeley and Los Angeles: University of California Press, 1968.

Marilyn L. Williamson, *Infinite Variety: Antony and Cleopatra in Renaissance Drama and Earlier Tradition.* New Haven, CT: Mystic, 1974.

Index

Picture Credits

About the Author

Historian and award-winning writer Don Nardo has written or edited numerous books about the ancient world, including *Empires of Mesopotamia*, *The Ancient Greeks*, *Life of a Roman Gladiator*, *The Pyramids of Egypt*, *Ancient Civilizations*, and the *Greenhaven Encyclopedia of Greek and Roman Mythology*. Mr. Nardo lives with his wife, Christine, in Massachusetts.